Walter Frewen Lord

The Lost Empires of the Modern World

Essays in Imperial History

Walter Frewen Lord

The Lost Empires of the Modern World
Essays in Imperial History

ISBN/EAN: 9783337173067

Printed in Europe, USA, Canada, Australia, Japan

Cover: Foto ©ninafisch / pixelio.de

More available books at **www.hansebooks.com**

THE LOST EMPIRES OF THE MODERN WORLD

Essays in Imperial History

BY

WALTER FREWEN LORD
AUTHOR OF 'THE LOST POSSESSIONS OF ENGLAND'

LONDON
RICHARD BENTLEY AND SON
Publishers in Ordinary to Her Majesty the Queen
1897
[All rights reserved]

CONTENTS

I.
INTRODUCTORY - - - - - 1

PAGE

II.
THE LOST EMPIRE OF PORTUGAL - - - 27

III.
THE LOST EMPIRE OF SPAIN - - - 95

IV.
THE LOST EMPIRE OF FRANCE - - - 171

V.
THE LOST EMPIRE OF HOLLAND - - - 287

VI.
CONCLUSIONS - - - - - 331

I.

INTRODUCTORY.

I.

INTRODUCTORY.

THE world is continually being reminded that in the arts of empire the English are mere plagiarists, stupid plagiarists who have spoilt what they have stolen. They have not, so it is affirmed, one single original or admirable quality. They were not great discoverers like the Portuguese, or a great Christianizing power like the Spaniards. They have not the art of conciliating natives like the French, nor even of making themselves beloved by their own colonists. They have not even the wits to make their empire pay like the Dutch. They roll up, everywhere, mountains of debt; they extort only that they may squander. The single quality that they possess in an abundant degree is neither rare nor original. Heavy bloodsuckers, they bestride the earth with their so-called empire like a nightmare; the world would be a sweeter place to live in without them; the amount of damage they have wrought is as wide as the realm that they have filched from their betters with so much violence and fraud.

These pleasantries, oft repeated, have grown to have the weight of arguments; and, indeed, they form a very ingenious substitute for argument. For, if one would answer them, it can only be done at the expense of much time and labour. Either one must travel and see for one's self whether or no the British Empire deserves this heavy indictment, or one must expend much time in research at home, in order to judge whether our predecessors and contemporaries merit such unqualified eulogium. Both courses take time to pursue with any measure of thoroughness, and travelling is not only a long task, but a very expensive one. Yet there are many English-speaking folk who are genuinely unable to give in their adhesion to the imperial idea, because their thoughts are so constantly disturbed by reflections like these; and perhaps by even harsher comments, to all of which they can get no reply, except one that varies from the 'retort courteous' to the 'lie direct.'

Neither the 'retort courteous' nor the 'lie direct' affords comfort to a troubled conscience; it must have facts. It is not a matter of very great difficulty to get at the facts; the requisite research, if wide, is not profound, and can be compassed by any man with a year's leisure at his disposal. But the number of men so fortunately placed is small, and most men with a year's leisure at their disposal prefer to spend it otherwise than in confuting, with so much labour, a troublesome political antagonist. Such men, we reflect, can always be voted down, British fashion, when the time comes; and in the meantime we may rest contented to differ from them.

But the man with a troubled conscience is not to be so put off; he is usually a man without great means or leisure, but before he votes he will know whether he is justified in voting. It is with a view to helping him to decide whether or not the British Empire is the thing of darkness that many would have us believe it to be that the present imperfect attempt at history is put forward. Four only of our predecessors in empire have been selected for study—Portugal, Spain, France and Holland. It may be well reasoned that there are but four European nations who have preceded us in this work; for although Genoa and Venice were mighty and wealthy States, they hardly rose to the position of what we understand to-day by an Empire. They were, rather, highly successful and sumptuous trading corporations. Their indifference to their neighbours was proverbial; and it was chiefly in consequence of her long-pursued policy of selfish isolation that Venice, when she fell, fell without a regret, and that her fall so little disturbed the polity of Europe, in spite of the fact that she had so long occupied a conspicuous, and sometimes a commanding position. Extension of territory was not much sought by these wealthy

Republics; and it is precisely extension of territory—extraordinary extension of territory—that is the great feature of all modern empires. Beyond the great days of Genoa and Venice we come to the Middle Ages, linked by the holy Roman Empire to the ancient world; none of which epochs have any lesson for the England of to-day.

The great extension of British territory that is known as the British Empire has, of course, largely been achieved at the expense of her predecessors; so that we shall have to consider whether the authority to which we have succeeded was more nobly exercised than our own, and also whether we displaced our predecessors in a manner so reprehensible that no conscientious man can honestly desire to see our empire endure any longer. Supposing the verdict of history to be, on the whole, in favour of England, we shall then consider what lessons we may draw from the efforts of our predecessors; and how far a contemplation of their successes and failures may help us to consolidate our own power.

The first European Empire of the modern

world in point of time was that of Portugal: it is also the most interesting. It was, almost exclusively, the handiwork of the Portuguese monarchs: in fact, we may say that the history of Portugal is the history of its kings. They were very wise kings, and the world was better for their work. There came a time, however, in the history of the royal stock, when the statesman merged in the fanatic. The change coincided with a critical period in the history of the empire, and proved to be an additional and most dangerous source of weakness. The collapse of Portugal followed with extraordinary rapidity, and she has never recovered her old position. Her former empire included what is now the Republic of Brazil and the Dutch East Indies; but what remains is still large enough to be called a Colonial Empire, and the question whether it is good for the world that that empire should grow and prosper must be answered in the affirmative.

With the exception of their religious fanaticism (and one must admit that that is a large exception) the Portuguese Empire was a clear gain to the world. It would be most desirable, in the interests of humanity, that the Portuguese should successfully develop their empire. There is not much room for further expansion either in India or Africa; but there is abundant room for development. On whatever lines that development took place, it would result in a realm of a very different type from any other now struggling to life in Africa; and that would be highly advantageous. Variety of excellence is more and more needed every day as the world is gradually overrun by mankind.

A revived Portuguese Empire is only a possible event if the Portuguese can make up their minds to follow their King. That is the plain lesson of history. As for supposing that there is any particular virtue in, for example, a republican form of government, that endows it with greater expansive force than it can hope to acquire while trammelled with the form of a monarchy, that is a mere figment of the historical theorist. Nor, seeing how serious are the troubles that follow a change of government, is it any longer honest to urge the experiment. The plain truth is, that what we call representative government suits England to perfection; and in a modified degree it suits some countries that are akin to us in blood. But it is startling to see how easily the machinery is thrown out of gear; and in Latin countries it has proved only a very moderate success. The East abhors it; and when we come to a Latin country in no small degree orientalized by infusions of Eastern blood, we are not surprised to find that it is practically a failure.

These are general reflections, and in the particular example of Portugal, history shows us that the country has really no chance of future greatness except from trusting itself to a leader. Fate has been kind to the country and has given her a King, who, in all human probability, ought to reign for another fifty years; if Portugal is to be mighty again, he must rule as well as reign. That is the simple issue before the Portuguese people. If they are contented with things as they are, it is well; but if they would have an empire, it is their King, and their King only, who can make it for them.

The extent of territory that was once Portuguese and is now English is very small. All the Eastern Archipelago went to the Dutch; but Ceylon was once Portuguese; although, inasmuch as it had been Dutch for many generations before we captured it, there is no reason to count it as a Portuguese colony lost to England. Goa, Diu and Daman we might have had over and over again had we chosen. They still remain Portuguese, and it is to be hoped that they will grow in wealth and strength. Why they are not English will be variously explained. Some will venture to assert that it is from the courtesy of the strong towards a temporarily enfeebled neighbour. Others will say that it is from obedience to some dark and cruel policy, the full iniquity of which has not yet been disclosed.

As regards our future relations, there is no reason why they should not be friendly, and even intimately friendly. Portugal has no grudges against England; England has no reason to be otherwise than sincerely glad at any change for the better in the outlook for Portugal. We are old allies by policy, and old connections by blood. What is often quoted as a drawback to the advance of Portugal, the infusion of foreign blood, is surely — considering the climates and the countries where her work must be carried on—an advantage; and no inconsiderable one. Whether Portugal will seize her opportunity is one of the most interesting problems of the day.

If Portugal has no reason to owe England a grudge, Spain has even some reason to exult over her. For if we have taken nothing from Portugal, we made two grand conquests, not to mention Gibraltar, from Spain — Cuba and the Philippines — and were compelled to restore them both under circumstances that must always be a source of pride to Spain rather than of discomfiture. There is, therefore, no reason why, in the future, we should not be as friendly with

Spain as with Portugal; our present interests do not clash, and there are no grounds for bitter feeling arising from past history. Before we quit this part of our subject, we must recall for a moment the Peninsular War. Surely, if ever one nation laid another under an obligation, England was, at the commencement of the century, in that position towards Spain and Portugal.

We now come to the question whether the Empire of Spain was a blessing or a curse to the world. It required for its foundation the mutilation of two great peoples, and the total obliteration of two highly interesting civilizations. This is an unpromising beginning; but it is usually excused on the ground that Spain converted her American subjects to Christianity. This, certainly, is an excuse that no Christian will undervalue. It demands a closer study of the history of the conquest; and, unfortunately, the more closely we examine it, the more deplorable it looks. Whether is the better, we ask ourselves, to be a pagan like the Inca, or to be a lamentable wretch of a Christian like

Pizarro? These mountains of corpses, these rivers of gore, are they, in very truth, fitting witnesses of the faith in whose name the mass is daily lifted heavenward, and the calvary stands by the roadside?

On the less debatable ground of political advantage we may perhaps find the justification of the conquest. Unfortunately the case is even clearer. Spanish South America is a by-word in modern times for disorder; and the nightmare of Spanish dominion lasted for three hundred years. If we inquire why it fell, the answer is, that it is a marvel that it endured as long as it did; for there really was no reason why it should stand. It had no cohesive force, and no principle of life. It was held together by sheer terror, by the menace of a relentless despotism acting from a vast distance over seas.

We must admit that the work of the conquest was done thoroughly: the terrorizing was complete. For Spain was in complete decadence for fully a century and a half before her dependencies dreamed of throwing off their allegiance; so fearful had been the lessons of the conquest. It appears, however, to be impossible to extirpate a breed of the force of the ancient Mexicans and Peruvians.

After two generations of disorder, something like settled government is now returning to South and Central America; the inspiration of which (in so far as can be seen with any degree of clearness through such a tangle) is chiefly Indian. But, however that may be, it seems abundantly clear that from the date of the conquest down to the revolt of the Spanish Colonies, there was no progress whatever made on the South American Continent; so that the net result of the Spanish Empire was to retard a continent for three centuries. As a set-off, the continent is, nominally at least, and perhaps more than nominally, Christian. If that be all in all, the claim of Spain as a civilizing power must rank very high; if there be any other duties that a nation has, then Spain must be confessed to have failed in all of them.

In effect, Spain was an Asiatic power of the old conquering, exterminating type. In all essential features of conduct there is nothing whatever to distinguish the Conquistadores from those numerous chieftains of Central Asia who have, throughout long centuries, gone forth from their highlands and steppes conquering and to conquer. Through seas of blood they waded to the domination of the gentler races of the South. Tartars and Seljuks and Moguls and Turks and Afghans have all founded, and in the ages to come, perhaps, many other races may found again, empires of the Spanish type. It is idle to assert that Spain should be marked off from these peoples by reason of her religion. Granted that the Spanish is religious, so is the Turk, deeply, fanatically religious. His revelation is different, but his spirit is the same.

It is a far cry from Baghdad to Lima, quite as far as from London to Calcutta; nevertheless, that is the track by which the East invaded the West, and even the Far West. The spirit of the Orient, sweeping along the north of Africa, desolating the churches on its way, crossed the narrow straits and entered Spain. After a conflict of many centuries, it was apparently expelled; but far from being thrust back into Africa, it had entered into the very soul of the Spaniard. Crossing the Atlantic, though by now it had changed its name and called itself Christian, it fell on the fair pagan dominions of America, as of old it had fallen on Persia and Mesopotamia, and repeated in Mexico the abominations of Tamerlane on the Tigris.

This is the grand invasion of the West by the East; just as the British Empire is the grand invasion of the East by the West. This is the broad distinction between Portugal and England on the one hand, and Spain on the other. Portugal (though sadly shorn of her glory) and England (still in the full tide of success) are of the West; Spain is of the East.

We now come to the lost Empire of France, which, in its potentialities, actually makes up the greater part of the British Empire; and we must not suppose that France will ever forgive us for having taken it away. There is, however, this reservation to be made, that the Colonial Empire of France was not a great national movement, so perhaps the resentment against England for its loss will not be either national or enduring; but that is rather a hope than a conviction. Still there remains the fact that in the past, as in the present, it is to the intelligence and the imagination of a few highly-placed men that France owed and owes her Colonial Empire; not to the eager rush of her sons to the uttermost parts of the earth. The sense of grandeur was perhaps, to a certain extent, national; but the loss and disappointment certainly were not.

The question of the capacity of France for colonizing is one of the extremest complexity. It seems hardly conceivable that a nation capable of so many and varied achievements should really be unable to colonize; and yet something like that conclusion is forced upon us by history. By slow degrees, and with infinite nursing, the French did indeed found one considerable colony of their own blood on the Saint Lawrence. All their other settlements outside France seem to have a certain flavour of artificiality. Even Canada is not a settlement of such freshness or distinctiveness as to make us feel that the world has suffered a loss in the check that French colonization received from England. When we come to empires founded on the domination of other races, the case is even stronger.

In days gone by, the French were conspicuous for the affection that they inspired in native races. It was the great distinction that marked them off from the English. The position appears to be reversed to-day.

None the less is France determined to persevere. Like England, she has lost one empire only to found another. England lost her American Colonies; but Australia, New Zealand, Tasmania, South Africa, and immense extensions in India, have far more than made up for that great loss. France lost Canada and the nascent Empire of India; she has, since the commencement of this century, acquired an immense territory in South Eastern Asia, another in Northern

Africa, another (which she hopes to unite to the first) in Western Africa, and quite recently the most important island of Madagascar. This is surely a mark of the most exuberant vitality. But it is even more astounding when we reflect that she is at the same time facing the greatest naval power on sea and the greatest military power on land; while bearing the burden of a national debt twice the size of that of England.

France has so often astonished the world that she may well do so again. But to face England and the Continent together proved to be too much for her in the days of Louis the Great, and too much for her again in the days of Napoleon the Great. To that task she has added to-day the burden of an immense empire over-seas. There are set-offs, assuredly; but the task is Titanic, nevertheless. The work of England is comparatively light.

If it be to the world's advantage that each nation should attain to its highest point of development, thus presenting to all other peoples the stimulating spectacle of great varieties of excellence, it is much to be regretted that so much of the former colonial Empire of France should have merged in that of England. The world would appear to have lost much in not possessing some realm outside France where Frenchmen have stamped the genius of their country on a new soil, and under new conditions.

But the idea of the loss is quite illusory; for, as a matter of history, France has never put her soul into her colonial enterprises, nor is she doing so to-day. Frenchmen are far too happy and contented in their own enchanting country to travel far afield. The grave and absorbing work of empire-making is irksome to a people so home-loving and affectionate. So, while the voice of ambition fitfully urges Frenchmen on to settle abroad, the voice of France is ever calling them home.

Although we can hardly expect Frenchmen to admit it, that kind of empire that most attracts them—the exercise of dominion over native kings and races—is what they appear to be even less suited for than colonizing by settlement. Egypt is the most complete demonstration of this position. The work was done, with the exception of the last touch. True, a minister hung back; but what of that? English ministers are always hanging back. It is not by one, or by a hundred incapable ministers—and England has had quite that number in her time—that a race is to be kept back that has empire in its blood.

So, though we may trace the loss of the French-Indian Empire to this source or the other, the teaching of history is very plain, that even if it had been safely founded, it could not have endured for long; and the probability is that it would eventually have become English in spite of the delay of a century, or perhaps a little more.

We now come to the last of our great predecessors—Holland, and we must draw a great distinction between the Dutchman at home and the Dutchman abroad, between Hollanders founding their independence and Hollanders founding their empire. The revolt of Holland against Spain is almost, if not quite, the noblest episode of modern history. It is largely to Holland that we of the North owe it that for three hundred years the desolating breath of Spanish tyranny has not come nigh our shores.

The Dutchman's protest in favour of civil and religious liberty is immortal, and until, as may duly happen in the course of centuries, the present stage of the world's civilization comes to its close, Holland must hold the first place among the liberators of the world. It is the more strange that a nation of such exalted patriotism, such warmth of religious feeling, and such a keen sense of justice, should display so little nobility when she enters on her grand period.

It was not that Holland was bloodthirsty; far, very far indeed, was Holland from that offence. It was simply that Holland 'sweated,' in the modern phrase, her dependencies. She set to work as if saying, 'Hollanders have had a hard life at home; they shall have an easy life now.' Her religious feelings do not seem to have restrained her from exploiting her Eastern subjects to the fullest possible extent. Rather, they seem to have stimulated her in carrying on her oppressions. The fierce old Hebrew sentiment 'The Lord hath delivered them into our hands' exactly describes her attitude. She 'worked them for all they were worth.'

Without employing this shop-keeping expression it is difficult to exactly describe how entirely the Dutch looked on their vast empire as a commercial enterprise. There was no question of raising the natives in material comfort or intellectual calibre; their sole reason for existing was that they might make fat fortunes for Dutchmen: so long as they were alive they could contribute to that end, and there was no other end to which they could contribute—no other end, at any rate, that a Dutchman cared to recognize.

The rebellion against Spain was the Dutchman's work; the founding of the empire was his pleasure; the Dutchman was grim in his pleasure. Holland, the noble little country, is, and must be for ever, a beacon to all who seek light for noble aim and noble endeavour; but the Dutch Empire, whatever it may be now, was an abominable exhibition of selfishness.

So, to return to the considerations with which this chapter commenced, the conscientious hesitator may surely take comfort from the contemplation of the lost empires that have preceded our own. The empire most like our own was that of Portugal; its downfall is to be deplored, and its revival hoped for. That of Spain was simply Asiatic, a mighty offshoot of the Orient, stretching out even across the Atlantic. It has fallen, as all Oriental empires fall, never to rise again. Other States may build on its ruins, but when once the flame has burnt out, there is no rekindling the ashes. Both these two were national enterprises, the one breathing the West, the other the East. But the lost empire of France was not a national enterprise; nor is the modern empire of France. Both, though mighty in extent, were of comparatively feeble vitality. They certainly were not of any damage to the cause of progress, but they, equally certainly, have not much inspiring force, being but artificial creations themselves.

The empire of Holland, though called an empire, was simply an immense commercial enterprise. It was conducted on the strictest, and even the sharpest, business principles. The vast enrichment of Hollanders is, no doubt, an agreeable result for Holland, but the process is not interesting or elevating to onlookers, and the means by which it was attained are generally condemned by all conscientious hesitators, being precisely those which England is most constantly and unfairly accused of employing.

Assuredly the British Empire is not perfect —nobody but a 'Jingo' would pretend that it was. But its existence is, on the whole, an advantage to the world, and it is far in advance of any of its predecessors, from whatever point of view we consider it. If it has benefited or enriched Englishmen, it has also benefited and enriched the men of other nations, and if it is ever to close its doors to them it will only be under foreign compulsion that it will do so.

II.

THE LOST EMPIRE OF PORTUGAL.

II.

THE LOST EMPIRE OF PORTUGAL.

M. DE CHAMFORT relates that when the English Ambassador at Lisbon was asked what was the difference between a Spaniard and a Portuguese, he replied, 'If you take away all a Spaniard's good qualities, what is left is a Portuguese.'

M. de Chamfort was a professional collector of good stories; and, of course, it was not to be expected that he should give up such a good illustration of British insolence from any pedantic scruples as to whether it was likely to be true or not. So he duly enshrined it in his collection: and the fable has no doubt contributed not a little towards the unfavourable view of the English character that prevails on the Continent.

But if the anecdote is a fable—as it almost certainly must be—the question is pertinent; and if the fable could ever have been narrated with anything approaching a semblance of truth, it was during the eighteenth century, the period to which Chamfort ascribes it, and at which date the Portuguese Monarchy touched its lowest point of feebleness. But the Portuguese Monarchy is a good deal older than the eighteenth century, and has a history of such not merely comparative, but absolute, grandeur and heroism that a mere moment of degradation — such as a generation or so of time in a life centuries long—may be made the occasion of a feeble joke, but cannot be made anything else if we are attempting to estimate a nation's qualities.

The men of our generation have no good reason to speak with respect of Portugal, unless they are members of the very small class of historical students. This is a commercial age: and Portugal has no claims to consideration on account of her commercial achievements, for she is chronically bankrupt.

Fighting has been always in fashion, but Portugal has done no fighting since the Peninsular War, where she certainly distinguished herself highly; but the overshadowing greatness of the Duke of Wellington has made us forget her achievements, although the Duke himself always did justice to them. This is an age in which every country prides itself on its internal administration and the security afforded to travellers, and Portugal, unfortunately, is not remarkable for either.

There is no surer sign of a country's real grandeur than a quick eye for great characters. In days gone by Portugal was conspicuous among the nations for knowing a great man when she saw one. It was not only that she did honour to her own great men (of whom she had a plentiful crop); not content with them, she welcomed with open arms the eager spirits of other nations who came to cast in their lot with hers.

No nation can long remain in this state of noble enthusiasm, so we need not inquire why Portugal no longer attracts and retains the services of accomplished foreigners. Such wide sympathies so widely indulged in make rare moments of grandeur in a nation's history.

But where are the great men of Portugal's own breeding to-day—the soldiers, above all, the colonial administrators? Such men there still must be in that land of heroic memories, and one very great man, at least, we know that there is. Inasmuch as in Portugal the destiny of the throne and the destiny of the people are one, we must, even at the risk of impertinence, recall the history of the years 1889 to 1897. The spirit of Henry the Navigator and John the Perfect is still there to guide the Portuguese if they have not yet quite lost their old infallible instinct for great men. Never had Portugal greater need of that instinct; let her look overseas. The Empire of Brazil has fallen; and the miserable Government that succeeded it has become a mere derelict, dangerous to others, incapable of directing itself. As to 'golden Goa,' let anyone who has sailed from Bombay down the western coast of India remember what 'golden Goa' was like—or even Panjim—and he will need a stronger dose of historic imagination than most men possess to enable him to realize that Portugal was once mighty and may yet be mighty again.

Of all the lost empires, that of Portugal is the most interesting, and the most fruitful in lessons to existing empires. And this not only because it was romantic to an unparalleled degree, but because in the conditions of its rise and its prosperity it more exactly resembles the British Empire than any other of the lost empires of history; and Englishmen, who seemingly know so well how to found empires, may, by studying the lost empire of Portugal, learn how best to avoid losing them. It is not much in the Englishman's way to learn from reading—he learns from experience mostly; but we cannot afford to learn from experience how empires are lost, so, if we would know, we must needs learn from history.

It seems to be the destiny of small kingdoms adjacent to mighty neighbours to be absorbed in the territory of the latter. Scotland merged in England, Burgundy in France—of late the process has gone on with extraordinary rapidity, and famous States and Monarchies have been absorbed by the dozen to make up the great empire of Germany, and, as some may think, the essentially greater kingdom of Italy. How comes it that Portugal remains independent of Spain? Unless—as men are only too apt to do—we hastily and superficially conclude that both Spaniard and Portuguese are worthless and worn-out types, and that Portugal is only not absorbed by Spain either because she is not worth absorbing, or because Spain has not the requisite strength or ambition—unless we are content with this entirely erroneous view, we shall have to conclude that some considerable difference between the two types does exist, and that the Portuguese has a native sturdiness that we have overlooked. This, or something like this, is the view that history leads us to. To appreciate the mighty Portuguese Empire, how it arose, and the forces that could overcrow its vigour, and produce its decline, we must perforce trace the Portuguese race to its source.

Portugal has no natural boundaries, like the Rhine, the Alps, or the Pyrenees, that seem to mark off certain territories for the habitat of different races. Everything was against the probability of a separate kingdom being carved out of the western portion of the peninsula; and the distinctive national existence of Portugal, as well as her subsequent expansion into an empire, is due to two causes: firstly, the vigour and sagacity of her rulers, whether as kings, or, later on, as emperors, in all but the name; and, secondly, the courage and tenacity of the people. So we come back to the question, What was the Portuguese people?

Without exhausting the subject, we may say that it was an amalgam of a pre-historic tribe and some Celtic invaders, strongly coloured with Roman influence and Latin blood, and overlaid by Visigoth.

So far, there is not much to distinguish the Portuguese from the early Briton; and the reproach—if it be a reproach—of 'mongrel,' which is freely levelled at the Portuguese by undiscerning critics, is perhaps less applicable to this race than to any other of the Aryan races of Europe. In the mouth of an Englishman, who is probably the greatest mongrel of Europe, and therefore the most successful of modern types, the epithet is particularly absurd. The difference between the British and the Portuguese type at the end of the fifth century A.D. probably amounted to this: that in Portugal the Roman element was the stronger, whereas in England various other invading strains combined with the native breed to overpower the Roman stock. The influence of the discipline of the Great Republic was equally great on the minds and habits of thought of the two peoples. But in Portugal Rome, in addition, stamped her impress on the language and the laws of the people, so that the Portuguese definitely entered the Latin family of nations while England remained definitely outside. The Phœnician colonies were never more than trading settlements, either in the Scilly Isles or at Carthagena, and, though there are more traces of Phœnicia in Portugal than in England, the sum total of Semitic influence was insignificant in either case.

When all is said, the Roman was a dull fellow. He was brave, fierce even; a good soldier and, according to his lights, a good citizen, if a coarse human being. But he lacked fire. In the arts and in literature he could only imitate; in science he invented nothing; commerce he despised. He was supreme in the one intellectual pursuit where hard and commonplace minds do mostly triumph—the study and practice of law. How comes it, then, that the Portuguese—up to the fifth century more Roman than anything else — distinguished himself in history by deeds which transcended the flights of the wildest imagination? Whence came the unrivalled tact with which he founded and governed successfully, and under the most varied conditions, empires in Brazil and the Indies? What turned Lisbon into the commercial capital of Europe, and produced the lofty literature of Camoens?

These are essentially romantic performances, and, though we derive our word 'romantic' from the city on the Tiber, romantic is the last thing in the world that any Roman either was or desired to be. He was of the earth, earthy.

The determining strain in the Portuguese race—the strain that decided its destiny—seems to have come from the desert.

The Saracens did not enter Portugal as invaders; they were invited over the Straits to be the make-weight in a domestic quarrel. But, once there, they founded kingdoms. They were not ardent proselytizers, and they took the greater hold of the country in consequence. There were numerous converts from Christianity to Islam, just as, later on, the process was reversed. But it must be confessed that the conversions to Islam have more the external appearance of willing conversions than those from Islam to Christianity. There were many of both kinds, throughout centuries. The Saracens made good and capable rulers; they brought a high, if somewhat exotic, civilization with them; they were tolerant and sumptuous. Portugal prospered under them, and the national character took a deep tinge of Saracenic culture and ideas, not only from the natural impulse to imitate and admire their rulers, but from the influence, at once more direct, more subtle, and more lasting, of constant intermarriage in all ranks of life.

Extreme precocity, both intellectual and physical, is the great feature of contrast between East and West. When the star of the East is in the ascendant, the results of this precocity seem almost miraculous to the Western mind.

The great Mussulman kingdom of Southern India was founded by a slave in an oasis, rose to a height of glory whose mere remains are the wonder and delight of travellers, decayed and fell into ruins—all within the period between Richard III. and James II. The Saracen dominion in Africa and Spain took somewhat longer to found and develop, and its decline was more gradual; perhaps for these reasons its influence persisted longer.

When the grasp of the Caliphate was relaxed, the Emirs of Portugal proclaimed themselves independent, and became, in their castles, in no way different, except in religion, from the Christian chiefs in their castles. Except in religion—there lay all the difference. That was an age of religious wars, and it was not to be expected that Moslem noble and Christian noble would settle down side by side, content with no more and no greater excitement than an occasional raid on each other's territory afforded. Had they been so easily satisfied, the civilization of Portugal would have developed on all fours with the civilization of Northern Italy—the Italy of the Montagus and Capulets, of Sforzas and Viscontis—it might have been as great, but it would have been no greater.

But Europe was aflame with religious, or pseudo-religious, zeal; and the chieftains of Portugal were soon arrayed, not, as everywhere else, each man against his neighbour, but Christian against Moslem. It was an age of knight-errantry. From all over Northern Europe came knight adventurers, with their trains of followers, great and small, to aid in the Holy War; and when the struggle was over, and the Portuguese people, burnt and hammered into unity, stood before the world as a nation, a new and valuable stock of Northern blood had found its way into the national amalgam.

The ultimate fate of Islam is made the subject of many facile speculations. It is customary to speak of the faith as 'decadent.' It is true that since the Turks were driven from the gates of Vienna the boundaries of Mussulman kingdoms have everywhere receded. Turkey in Europe has dwindled to one-sixth of her size at the commencement of this century. Her former fiefs along the southern shore of the Mediterranean have mostly fallen under Christian domination. Persia has grievously dwindled in power and population.

All this no doubt represents a period of serious retrogression that has already endured for two centuries. And as faith and conquest are closely allied in the creed of Islam, the waning of faith is followed by a more plain diminution of temporal authority than would attend a similar lukewarmness among Christians. Probably the present languor of Islam is not greater than the languor of Christianity in the seventeenth and eighteenth centuries, and against this languor we have to set two great facts. The first is the rapid and steady progress made by Islam in Central and Western Africa, where Mussulman missionaries are yearly gaining over whole tribes of excellent fighting material to the creed of Mahomet. The second is the Mahdist revolt in Eastern Africa. By the efforts of England this revolt has now been rounded off into an episode. But the rise of the Mahdi was exactly one of those volcanic movements which have before now changed the face of continents, and may do so again. Undoubtedly, if it had not been for England, the Mahdi would have overrun Egypt, Turkey in Asia, and even if he had been turned back from Constantinople his government might have had an indefinite expansion into Central Asia. It was from one of these outbursts of heroic endeavour, and the answering exaltation called forth from Christendom, that the kingdom of Portugal was born.

When William of Normandy was parcelling England among his knights, the Portuguese tribes, a sturdy remnant, were struggling for dear life against the Moslem, and bravely holding their own in the northern provinces of what we now call Portugal. Their feeble ones had long since been weeded out by war, and much of their country depopulated. Those that remained were hardy, simple folk, pious without bigotry, excellent husbandmen, excellent men of the chase, excellent warriors.

Besides this assemblage of native virtues, they had drawn from the blood of their enemies the seeds of an adventurous and romantic temper. All that they needed to mould them into a mighty nation was a leader. He came to them from Northern Europe: Henry, a Burgundian Crusader, married to a daughter of their over-lord of Gallicia, by whom he had a son, Affonso. These were the first leaders of the Portuguese, the moulders of their character on national lines, the founders of their monarchy. Count Henry brought the daring, restless spirit of the Crusader; his wife brought personal charm and administrative ability; their son united their good qualities, and founded the royal line of Portugal.

It is no part of our subject—'The Lost Empire of Portugal'—to trace the further history of the little State, for little in extent of European territory it always remained. But, accustomed as we are to see in the Portugal of to-day a feeble and unsuccessful people, and in their possessions overseas unimportant posts, and territories hard to keep and hardly worth the keeping, we almost involuntarily ascribe to the Portugal of other days the same or similar characteristics. We are tempted to think that if Portugal ever conquered it must have been because their enemies were even feebler folk than themselves. In short, we do not realize the Portuguese Empire. The first step to that desirable end is to realize the Portuguese character as it was before it embarked on its great enterprises, and to understand that when the great age of Portugal began it found a nation numerically small, but morally and intellectually the first of its age, and governed by a dynasty that produced fewer incapable monarchs than any other seated on the thrones of Europe.

Portugal, naturally enough, did not immediately expand into an empire. Two problems had to be solved at home first. One was to make the kingdom of Castile recognize that she could not have the whole peninsula to herself; the other was to conquer the Algarves from the Moors. Both problems had to be solved by force of arms, and took three centuries to settle. The beginning of the fifteenth century found England and Portugal in close alliance. King John, the first ruler of the house of Aviz, had married a daughter of John of Gaunt. Naturally, his sympathies were Lancastrian, and Henry IV., in return for his prompt recognition by Portugal as King of England, had made King John a Knight of the Garter. It is agreeable and interesting to historic students to remember that King Carlos of Portugal recently received the Garter from his cousin, the Queen of England.

These are not trifles; or, if there be any so dour-minded as to maintain that the orders of knighthood are trifles, any student of history will admit that they often furnish him with valuable clues. One or other of the orders has always had a certain pre-eminence, so that to hold it is the natural incident to the sovereignty of a great State, or a mark of the highest personal distinction. At one time one would have inquired, Has he the Golden Fleece? at another, Has he the order of the Holy Ghost? at another, Has he the Garter?

John the First was proud of his Blue Ribbon. Definitely recognized, although a bastard, as one of the great European sovereigns, ruler of a compact nation, and himself a man of great abilities, even King John could have had no idea of the glory that awaited his dynasty and his nation in the course of the next century and a half.

John was proud of his English alliance, and named his eldest son Edward, after Edward III. of England. All his sons were brave and enterprising. Their model and idol was their cousin Henry, the victor of Agincourt. They were five most remarkable princes: four were men of action, one— Henry—a man of thought.

The eldest, Edward, pondered much over his duties as king, and was, perhaps, led astray by his desire to increase his own authority when he succeeded to the crown. Two of the others, Peter and Ferdinand, were knights-errant of the Crusading type, and their energies produced two great events: one a triumph, the capture of Ceuta; the other a disaster, the miserable attack on Tangier. But success and failure alike stimulated the longing of the daring Portuguese for enterprise abroad, and fed the enthusiasm on which Henry, the greatest of them all, calculated.

Henry the Thinker he should have been called. He is known as Henry the Navigator, although he never made a sea voyage.

In him the practical temper that he inherited from his English mother was informed by the resolute profundity which is characteristic of southern types at their best. He saw, no less than his father and his brothers, what a mighty engine the Portuguese nation had become. But he saw, what they did not see, that the energies of Portugal would be far more usefully employed in exploration and discovery than in romantic endeavours to exterminate Islam or to conquer Spain. Both of these were hopelessly impossible tasks— and useless tasks. And yet, unless some other outlet were found for the energy of Portugal, it would most indubitably be turned to one or both of these tasks, and that at once.

He wasted no time on words. He lost no time in pleasure or travel. He might have loitered away his time agreeably enough, for he would have been welcomed and fêted magnificently at all the courts of Europe, not only for his father's sake, but for his own. Instead, he settled down at Sagres, by Cape St. Vincent, the southernmost point of

Portugal, where he could daily look out on the sea that led to India. His local influence was unbounded, for he was Governor of the Algarves. Like his father and brothers, he was a Knight of the Garter. His appointment to the Algarves dated from 1419, and for forty-one years after that date, until his death in 1460, he never ceased to direct the expeditions that were fitted out under his orders for the discovery of the route to India. Forty years seems a long time, and when we consider that he died forty years before the route was discovered, we are at some loss whether to marvel most at the Prince's pertinacity or the sailors' courage. Without charts, without soundings, ignorant alike of the climate and of the ocean-currents with which they would have to deal, they put forth in open or half-decked boats into the Unknown.

On their return they visited their Prince, and told him what they had done. All were welcomed and rewarded. If a man got no further than his predecessors, his voyage at any rate confirmed, perhaps corrected, the experience of others. Any new facts were eagerly noted; discoveries might even be made, and perhaps earned for the daring navigator the honour of knighthood from Prince Henry's own hands — an honour coveted by all Europe.

At home the Prince planned and watched, drew up charts, studied every possible improvement in boat-building or compass, interviewed travellers, sought out daring sailors, guided, comforted, controlled. Many men thought him a dreamer, some even a dangerous dreamer. His own family, however, were all-powerful, and if they did not support him very eagerly, at any rate they took an interest in his pursuits. If they could not be entirely weaned from their dreams of conquering Spain and Morocco, they, at any rate, allowed the Prince to have his own way, and gradually results were forthcoming.

Years passed by, and the steadfast Prince continued collecting facts and travellers' tales, and sending out new so-called 'expeditions,' which only meant a handful of resolute men in a boat about the size of a first-class Deal lugger, and nothing like so seaworthy. So much of Africa was opened up in this way that the route to India, from being a personal hobby, grew to a provincial and then to a national enterprise. The first point that Prince Henry aimed at was the discovery of a sea route to Senegambia, to cut out the caravans that proceeded thither from Tunis. This does not seem a very considerable achievement, for Cape St. Vincent is in N. Lat. 36°, and Cape Verde is in N. Lat. 12°, but twenty-six years passed before Nuño Tristam passed the Senegal.

At first the grand object of all the sailors employed by Prince Henry was to round Cape Bojador, and fifteen years must pass before even this modest addition could be made to the geography of Western Africa. But they began well, for in the year after Prince Henry was appointed Governor of the Algarves, his men made the important discovery of the island of Madeira. Then came nothing but disappointment after disappointment. The most that his men could do was to reach one or another of the Canary Islands, and Cape Bojador still remained a forbidding, almost a legendary, promontory.

At last, in 1434, it was re-discovered and doubled. The next year they sailed 150 miles further; in 1436 210 miles further still, landed, and (for the first time) cast anchor, and essayed to gain the interior and find the trade routes; but that had to be given up after some skirmishing with the natives. So far, the Prince's work had gone on with very little interruption, but about this time the Tangier expedition was planned. Prince Henry made no remonstrances, or very few. In truth, achievements in his own line of exploration had hitherto been but unimportant. For seventeen years of work and thought he had nothing to show that would dazzle or convince the world. The first captains whom he had sent to sea were already grizzled veterans, if they were not dead, and the sea route to India was still a dream, a hobby of his Highness's, and not to be compared with the excitement of a campaign in Morocco. But, as soon as the war-fever had been stilled by copious blood-letting, and the Portuguese, appalled at the fearful disaster, were mourning the loss of their beloved Prince Ferdinand, left a captive with the Moors, the steadfast Prince Henry resumed his labours, and in 1441 Tristam made the important discovery of Cape Blanco. Two years later Nuño Tristam sailed twenty-five miles further south.

In 1445 the Prince resolved on a bold stroke. He entrusted a larger expedition than usual to Gonsalo de Cintra, with orders to proceed straight to Guinea without putting in. The expedition was a complete failure; but another, under Nuño Tristam, succeeded in the comparatively humble attempt to pass the Senegal. The next year Diniz Diaz, greatly daring, never struck sail till he had passed the Senegal. When he landed he found that the native type had changed; they were no longer the Moors that he and his were accustomed to fight and trade with. He had made a great discovery, for he had entered the land of the negroes. He discovered Cape Verde. There was, by this time, a keen rivalry among all the captains of Portugal for who should get furthest and deserve best of his Prince. In the same year that Diaz rounded Cape Verde, Nuño Tristam closed his last voyage with a brilliant triumph, for he got 300 miles further than Diaz, but was killed by a poisoned arrow while attempting to ascend the Rio Grande. In 1446, too, Alvaro Fernandes outdid even Nuño Tristam, for he nearly reached Sierra Leone. This was the best year of Prince Henry's life. By this date over fifty vessels had been on voyages of exploration more or less important. Nearly a thousand natives from different parts of the coast had been brought back to Portugal. The nation was agog with excitement and curiosity; the ocean had no more terrors for them. The impossible had already been overcome, the realm of dreams lay open to them; the great Prince's work was done. He had paved the way for the Portuguese Empire. He had given the people a new ambition. To be adventurers, navigators, explorers ; to open, enjoy, and revel in the new worlds before them — this was the ambition of the Portuguese. What was the ambition of the Englishman or the Italian at the same period?

In 1460 Prince Henry died ; but Portugal was now launched on the road to Empire. His work is well estimated by the royal order of 1469 granting privileges to Guinea traders ; and in which it was made a principal condition to the enjoyment of these privileges that one hundred leagues of the coast of Africa should be opened up every year. Exploration was recognized by the highest authority in the land as the manifest duty and prerogative of the Portuguese. Could any such order have emanated from the Sovereign in the year when, after the Ceuta expedition, Prince Henry was appointed Governor of the Algarves?

It is not to be supposed that the Portuguese could only grasp one idea at a time ; or that they succeeded merely by dogged perseverance in one line of discovery. A very versatile race was the Portuguese. Their minds took new impressions quickly; their energy was almost inexhaustible, and it was readily turned in a new direction when old directions were clearly no longer profitable. Fortunately, the men at the helm of the State were wise princes. Prince Henry the Thinker was now indeed dead, but his spirit lived. The direction of the work of exploration remained in the hands of the royal family, and in 1486 John the Perfect sat on the throne of Portugal. It was evident to him that although India might eventually be reached round the south of Africa it would take a very long time to discover the route. Certainly that line of discovery must be persevered in; but it would be better to start other lines as well.

For a good many years past there had been a revival of those early rumours concerning the land of Prester John, which, by all accounts was worth discovering. It was now placed by common consent in Abyssinia, and two expeditions were fitted out in 1486 with the object of getting there. The first, with daring originality, was ordered to sail up the Senegal to its source, evidently with the idea that the source of the Senegal would prove to be near enough to the boundaries of Abyssinia for the expedition to make its way on. The King's notion of direction was correct enough; but in point of distance he was out about 3,000 miles; so that this expedition got nothing but the honour and glory of being the first explorers of the Senegal.

The other expedition, not less daringly conceived, had momentous results. It was directed to sail along the Mediterranean, and then work overland to the Red Sea, and thence to Suakim, where apparently the explorers were to inquire their way. The first expedition failed because the officers composing it, not knowing Arabic, found that it would be useless to proceed further. It was followed by the expedition of Payva and Covilham. They both died in Abyssinia, which country was early reached by Affonso da Payva, who kept that one object steadily in view from the outset of their joint expedition. Covilham himself heard rumours on the way that showed him how much more glorious discoveries lay before him if only he could hold out. He reached Aden, where his restless and adventurous mind was finally made up by the news he heard of India. He made an extraordinary voyage, reached Cananore, on the Malabar coast, and saw Calicut and Goa. On the African coast he put in at Sofala. Here he heard about Madagascar (called the Island of the Moon), and also heard enough about the geography of Africa south of Sofala to entitle him to consider himself as the virtual discoverer of the Cape route.

One would think that this was renown enough for an ordinary man, but Covilham was an adventurer of the most exalted type. He made his way back to Cairo, and found Payva's messengers, the survivors of his expedition, without much difficulty. From them he learnt that Payva had died in Abyssinia, and had sent them to Cairo to await Covilham, and return to Portugal with him. This was all very well, but Covilham had a mind to see Abyssinia for himself. No doubt if he had been endowed with a more Northern sense of duty, he would have returned at once. Strictly speaking, he ought to have done so, but perhaps he thought that his message would atone for some shortcomings. So he sent back the survivors to Portugal with this message:

'Let the Guinea explorers persevere, let them sail ever South and fear not. When the time came that they must needs follow the land North, let them ask for Sofala and the island of the Moon. Here they shall find news of me; and as I crossed from India to Sofala, no doubt they will be able to return from Sofala to India.'

So the message went home, and Covilham turned back and started for Abyssinia. He never returned to Portugal, but his fate was not an unhappy one. At the capital of the King he was received kindly. It was a Christian country, and he settled there, entered the King's service, and died what we might call Prime Minister of Abyssinia. It is evident that in Covilham's nature there was (and small blame to him) a deep vein of personal ambition. True, he had disobeyed his monarch in that, having discovered Abyssinia, he did not return and report his success, but he may have reflected that the discovery of Abyssinia was, after all, a trifling matter beside the discovery of India; and had he not sent home to his Sovereign such information as was beyond the wildest hopes of any who strove to make the country mighty? Might he not now with justice profit himself? At any rate, he did so, and ended at the court of Abyssinia a life of wilder romance than an Arabian tale.

John the Perfect, in whom the spirit of Henry the Thinker survived in all its force, encouraged foreigners at his court — or, rather, it would be more accurate to say, he encouraged talent. What he wanted was ability, and if a man had brains, he need not fear lack of employment because his father had not been a Portuguese.

Cadamosto, a Venetian, had done much

good work for Prince Henry, and at the court of King John (Prince Henry's grand-nephew) there was often to be seen another Italian—a Genoese. It seems that he had a new plan for reaching India. King John liked new plans. He had a plan of his own for reaching Cathay by the north of Europe, in pursuance of which Martin Lopes discovered Nova Zembla. He had another plan for exploring Africa, in pursuance of which his messengers succeeded in discovering Timbuctoo.

We have seen how daringly he had schemed to reach Abyssinia by sailing up the Senegal, and by sailing down the Red Sea, and we shall soon see how gloriously his perseverance in despatching expeditions down the coast of Africa was to be rewarded. The Genoese may therefore have well reckoned on a favourable reception of his own plan for discovering India. The King received him very kindly, for the man was known as a daring fellow, who had already made voyages down the Guinea Coast in the Portuguese service. But as the plan was unfolded, the King became more and more shy of committing himself to it. On the difficulties of ocean-voyaging, and the best way of adapting resources to overcoming them, there was no greater authority living than the King of Portugal. But there were some points about this new plan which the King could see no way to meeting, and as to which the adventurer could offer no opinion except his conviction that the thing could be done.

The King made up his mind that the plan was impracticable. Perhaps a certain exaltation of manner on the part of the Genoese contributed to this unfavourable view, for he was at last told that the King had no time for dreamers, and the man left the Portuguese court to carry his plan elsewhere. His name was Christopher Columbus. So it seems to have been written in the book of Fate that Portugal was not to have all the glory that the world had to offer. But she already had much, and was soon to have more.

One Diaz, of a race of sailors and adventurers, was fitted out in 1486 with two ships, fairly large ones as ships went at that time— fifty tons apiece—and despatched to the Guinea Coast with orders (most sagacious orders!) to put in at the different well-known ports, and land at each one of them some of the natives who had been carried to Portugal from the coast of Africa by earlier expeditions. These natives were to tell their own tale of how they had been treated in Portugal, and what the Portuguese nation was like.

This most statesmanlike measure would suffice, even if we had no other evidence, to prove that the Portuguese possessed the instinct of Empire. They knew that they could only rule through the confidence felt in them by their subjects, and they began very early in their days of empire to win that confidence. Diaz's stock of ambassadors of goodwill was exhausted long before he reached the Orange River. Here his troubles began. He had to face the Unknown, and in his little craft of fifty tons was carried far south beyond the Cape into seas growing (to their alarm), not only rougher, but every day colder.

At length the wind turned, and he beat north, finally landing in Algoa Bay. He had turned the Cape at last, but he had turned the Cape without seeing it. At Great Fish Bay his crew mutinied, and compelled him to turn back. It was on his return journey that he first saw Table Mountain, christened by him, in memory of his buffeting, the Cape of Storms, but ever since known by the name bestowed on it by his grateful King—the Cape of Good Hope.

So it could be done. After seventy years of thought and study and trial, seventy years' application of the maxim of the great captain who died four hundred years after him, 'Erst wägen, dann wagen,' Diaz laid open the route to the East. There was now no doubt that the Indies could be reached round the Cape, and ten years later this was achieved.

One is so sated with wonders in reading early Portuguese history that the famous voyage of Vasco da Gama seems almost

commonplace. He left Portugal on July 8,
1497, in command of four vessels, the largest
being of 120 tons burden. He circum-
navigated Africa, and crossed the Indian
Ocean from Melind to Calicut, which place
he reached in May, 1498. From Great
Fish Bay to Mombasa he was practically
exploring for the first time, as Covilham, his
predecessor, had left no notes to guide him.
He returned to Lisbon at the end of August,
1499.

So ends the story of the discovery of the
East by Portugal, a story which it has been
necessary to trace in some slight detail in
order that we might understand what manner
of men the Portuguese were. The story of
the foundation of their Eastern Empire and
of its expansion is remarkable enough, but
is almost commonplace beside the story of
how the Portuguese got there. We must
content ourselves with remembering that to
found and govern a great empire the same
qualities have been required in all ages.
The Portuguese showed that they possessed
these qualities in ample measure—courage

and daring in war, skill in administration, uprightness in all things, judicial and fiscal. By 'empire' one means, of course, a settled State, and not the violent and precarious dominion of a predatory horde; for the making of which in all ages nothing much is needed beyond recklessness as to your own throat, and greater recklessness as to your neighbour's.

It is usually supposed that the Portuguese Empire in the East consisted of dominions on the western coast of India—of which three fragments remain, Goa, Daman and Diu—and of little else. But on their road to India they had founded what promised to be a considerable empire on the east coast of Africa. They were, in fact, dominant over the whole of that coast, and only natural obstacles prevented them from reaching the interior. The tribes with whom they contended were savages, and much milder savages than the Zulus or Matabele. Compared to the difficulties that awaited the Portuguese in India, the difficulties that confronted them in Africa were trivial, with the exception of two—malarial fever and the tsetse fly. The fever killed the men, and the fly killed the cattle. The Portuguese were continually struggling against these difficulties without realizing how great they were. With our extended knowledge we can see that they were attempting an impossible task. Had they worked their way up from the Cape, as we are doing now, and from a station inland pushed down to the sea, they would have had some chance of success; but they do not seem to have thought of such a course; and had they done so they would have been too few to have pursued it profitably. So the Portuguese Empire in Africa remained unimportant, except as a post on the road to India, and was probably at no period of its existence so flourishing as it is at the present moment.

But besides their settlements along the East Coast of Africa, the Portuguese had a wealthy station at Ormuz, on the Persian Gulf, by means of which they tapped the trade of Persia. They even held Aden for a year, and were only driven out by the

Turks. What the Turks were doing *dans cette galère* is a question, the answer to which shows in the most graphic manner possible how the grasp of Portugal had shaken the world. The Turks were there as the allies of their ancient foes, the Venetians, who had stirred them up against the Portuguese by pointing out the danger that Portuguese settlements in the East might prove to be to the Sultan. With all the advantages of geographical position, of prior possessions, and of accumulated wealth, the Venetians, terrified at the rapid decline of their profits, could devise no means of grappling with the stout-hearted adventurers from the Tagus, except setting against them the huge machinery of their common foe, the Ottoman Empire. As regards Aden that sufficed, but the Portuguese were not to be driven from Ormuz.

An immense and precious trade with the far East was set up by the settlement of Malacca. The Portuguese were the first Europeans in Madagascar, the Mauritius, the Maldives, Sumatra, the Moluccas, Siam, and Arakan, and when one says the first Europeans there, one does not imply that they merely put in, or even that they surveyed and noted down the countries and peoples of the East. They settled, signed treaties, established factories, opened up the countries to trade, and in some cases even attained to some measure of local sovereignty, after the fashion of Rajah Brooke. Every fresh point reached was regarded by them, primarily, as the starting-point for the next.

The more one studies, the more astounded one becomes at the sagacity and vitality shown by the explorers; and in even greater measure at the profundity of a mind like Prince Henry's, that could direct so mighty a current of human force from the easy, the pious, the glorious, but entirely futile task of slaughtering Moslems or Spaniards, and set it flowing along courses dark and perilous, fraught with every danger to man known and unknown, and in which, for three-quarters of a century, there seemed neither profit nor comfort, nor hope of profit or comfort. Indeed, much that the Portuguese achieved is almost incredible. When we reflect on the difficulty with which Europe has in our own time opened up communications with Japan and China, it is scarcely credible that Portugal had achieved this object by individual effort, and apparently with little difficulty, as early as the reign of Edward VI.

I have ventured the position that the lost empire of Portugal is more like the British Empire than any other empire that preceded the latter. It was founded as a commercial enterprise, and thence expanded into a military occupation, in precisely the same manner as the British Empire. There was this difference, that, whereas the British Empire was founded by private tradesmen, the Portuguese Empire in India was the undertaking of the sovereign. The kings and princes of Portugal had been its chief inspiration from the commencement, and it was only reasonable that, as they had borne the entire risk, they should take the lion's share of the profits. At its height the Portuguese Empire in India comprised Diu and Daman and the considerable settlement of Goa, all of which the Portuguese still retain. They had numerous other settlements on the Malabar coast, the complete domination of the island of Ceylon, and outposts at Ormuz and on the Húgli. These, together with the settlements on the coast of Africa, constituted their empire in the East.

* * * * *

We have now to consider their settlements in the West, the great self-governing colony of Portugal, afterwards the Empire, and now the Republic of Brazil.

We saw that Vasco da Gama reached Lisbon at the end of August, in the year 1499, on his return from his voyage round the Cape to India. The point on the Western Coast of India where it was decided to make the principal settlement for trade purposes was Calicut. The goodwill of the Rajah of Calicut must be conciliated as the first step towards opening up a trade with India. No time was lost in selecting a commander for this important mission, and in fitting out his ships. One would naturally expect that

Vasco da Gama would have been selected; but the King was jealous of Vasco da Gama. Portugal had seen the last of her great kings, and was very near her decline when Pedro Alvares Cabral was appointed Admiral of the new Indian Fleet. Not that Cabral was incompetent, but the passing over of Da Gama shows a littleness in high places that we are not accustomed to in reading Portuguese history.

It is open to question whether Cabral meant to discover Brazil or not. If he was as wary as he was daring, he probably took warning by the neglect of Da Gama, and wisely kept his counsel. It seems remarkable that, of the many score navigators who had left Portugal for the East, not one, in the eighty years of adventure that preceded Cabral's voyage, had encountered an easterly storm of any violence in the neighbourhood of Cape Verde. Such, however, was Cabral's version of what happened to him. He encountered a storm of such fury that it blew him across the Atlantic, and compelled him to anchor in a new land, at a place that he gratefully christened Porto Seguro. It was not until he had refitted, after discovering Brazil, that he proceeded on the comparatively humdrum journey to the East Indies, with his presents for the Rajah of Calicut.

Of course it is quite possible that the discovery of Brazil was a lucky accident, but it seems more likely that a man of Cabral's capacity and daring was not without designs. He found himself unexpectedly in command of a first-rate fleet. Eight years only had passed since Columbus had earned an immortal name by crossing the Atlantic. Why should he not do something in the same line? Of course he must say nothing about his intention, for the example of Da Gama showed only too clearly what a suspicious mind was his master's. Still, there could be no harm in succumbing to an adverse wind, and so Brazil was discovered.

It was a very long time before Brazil was considered to be a place of any importance. Even the grasping ambition of Spain left Portugal in undisturbed possession of the coast-line from Maranham to the River Plate

—apparently in indifference as to what they might be abandoning. Indeed, there was nothing to strike the imagination in Brazil. There were no ancient monarchies, such as those that confronted Pizarro and Cortez; no pushing energetic captains like the Adil Shahis, who were founding the noble city of Bijapur when the Portuguese settled in Goa. The gold and the diamonds were discovered later, and cast an after-glow of splendour over the Portuguese monarchy in the days that followed the Captivity. But at first there was nothing to report, except the discovery of a well-watered, fertile-looking country, not unlike their own Portugal, inhabited by races of gentle savages, primitive and inquisitive, almost without arms—quite without clothing—and destitute of political institutions. This land soon began to be settled and colonized by thrifty Portuguese immigrants, and was destined to be the mainstay of the monarchy for long after the time when Holland and England had snatched her Eastern possessions from her failing grasp.

Was Portugal, then, swarming with a population seeking an outlet? Are we to understand that Brazil was to Portugal what the self-governing colonies of England would be to the population-laden mother-country, if they rightly understood their own interests?

Unfortunately, it was not so. The whole population of Portugal at the present moment does not exceed the population of London. Four hundred years ago, it would probably be excessive to put it at three millions, of whom not one could be spared, if their native land was to be properly cultivated and defended. The colonization of Brazil was the result, not of a surplus population at home, but of two causes: one, persecution; the other, a state of things in the Southern provinces of Portugal which must be separately examined; and both subjects bring us face to face with the collapse of the Portuguese Empire.

To say that an event is 'inevitable,' is an easy way of getting out of the difficulty of inquiring into its causes. The word is much used in England, where we are somewhat impatient of thinkers, and of people who ask 'why' and 'wherefore.' Thus we hear of the 'inevitable' separation of England and America, whereas England has surmounted many and many a difficulty, far more complicated than the simple disputes between herself and the thirteen colonies. Thirty years ago we heard a good deal about the 'inevitable' break-up of the British Empire, but a little thought and courage (perhaps twice as much as would have bound us to America for ever) has made a considerable change in men's ways of speech on Imperial matters. Any time since 1874 we have heard men say, 'Home Rule must come, it is inevitable.' Is it, indeed? we may truly inquire in 1897.

A little thought and a little courage have marvellously changed men's minds in this respect. And so we have heard of the 'inevitable' triumph of Protestantism, and the 'inevitable' downfall of the English Church; neither of which events seems so certain as they both once appeared to be to the 'inevitable' order of mind. And it is quite of a piece with this somewhat slipshod method of historical dissertation that men should write and speak of the 'inevitable' collapse of the Portuguese Empire. Its collapse was no more 'inevitable' than its foundation.

The natural destiny of Portugal would seem to have been that it should develop into a sort of Italy, with numerous semi-independent lords of the soil, each reigning in his own small territory; or, perhaps, that it should have waxed great by the absorption of territory from Castile, so that the Peninsula would in the end have been divided between Portugal and Spain into less unequal portions than it is at present. The Portuguese, although they had a long coast-line, were not early conspicuous as mariners. More than fifty years before Prince Henry settled at Sagres, the English had fought and won their first great naval battle at Sluys. But even when Prince Henry the Thinker took up the work of exploration, his countrymen required a great deal of coaxing and persuasion, abundant praise and lavish rewards, in order to keep them up to the mark. They were not very bold or adventurous navigators at first. They were ignorant of boat-building and the use of the compass. It needed a man with the divination of a seer, as well as the inflexible will of a born captain of men, and endued by nature with the kindly and winning temper of the early Portuguese, to guide his country along the dark and dangerous paths of ocean discovery.

Thought founded the Portuguese Empire. If we would discover why it collapsed, we must consider its weak points. The fatal weakness was that Portugal had an unscrupulous and unfriendly neighbour, whose territory was separated from its own by no natural boundaries. So long as Castile and Aragon remained distinct kingdoms, there was little to fear: Portugal was nearly as strong as either, separately, and it was improbable that they would combine. But from the moment when the two crowns were united by the marriage of Ferdinand and

Isabella, it became a very grave danger to Portugal that she had contented herself with her original boundaries. Sooner or later, it was certain that Spain would attack Portugal; and to prepare for that attack would be the first work of any statesman or monarch who cared for his country's independence.

It did not call for a prophet to see this much. The facts were under the King's nose, and to prepare against them demanded nothing but thought and a few administrative orders. In the first place, it would have been plain to any thinker who was planning the salvation of his country that Imperial expansion had gone on somewhat too rapidly, considering the size of the mother-country. It is true that that expansion had made Lisbon the commercial capital of Europe, and had poured rivers of wealth into the country. But just at that moment steel and iron and men would have been of more value to Portugal than gold. Whence could she draw them? Well, there were two ports in the East, Ormuz and Húgli, which could have been abandoned without endangering the rest of the empire.

Ormuz, like Aden, had been occupied by Albuquerque, with the idea of closing the Red Sea to the commerce of Venice—corking it up, as we should say now. It was a grandiose scheme, like all Albuquerque's schemes, but it was essentially an offensive move, not necessary to the proper defence of the Eastern Empire. How little danger there was of aggression from this direction is shown by the fact that Ormuz was not stormed by the Persians until 1626, or forty-six years after the first year of Captivity. Húgli was an important fort and trading centre that occupied a very large garrison when it fell to the Moguls in 1629. Portugal lost 5,000 men there. It was much too far off Goa to be anything but a weakness to the empire. Certainly, a considerable loss of income would have followed on its abandonment, but what Portugal wanted was not income but men. The garrisons of Ormuz and Húgli being withdrawn to Portugal would have represented an addition of several regiments to the home army.

We now come to Goa. It had been one of the great Albuquerque's plans to encourage marriage between the men of the Goa garrison and the native women. His idea was to build up a population that should be wholly Portuguese in sentiment, and that could be relied on to make a fine army for defence, and perhaps for aggression. A great idea, certainly, but a wrong one in essence, because the offspring of these unions proved to be not good for much. But without entering into the question of the fighting qualities of the half-caste, the settlement of the Goa garrison ought to have been strictly forbidden, and a term of years fixed for service in the East, after which the garrison would be withdrawn to the mother country.

The increased population was not needed in India, as was shown by the severe defeats that the small garrison had over and over again inflicted on the armies of Bijapur, and by withdrawing the troops to Portugal after five years' service the King would have added another three or four regiments to his home army. Diu and Daman were strong places, and the island of Ceylon, with its wealthy trade, could easily have been retained and defended, as Portugal was now a first-rate naval power. Moreover, by the abandonment of Ormuz and Húgli the duties thrown on the navy would have been considerably lightened. Thus pruned, and its strength concentrated, the Portuguese Empire in India would have been practically impregnable. In Africa, if the same or similar measures had been adopted, another regiment would have been saved, and many precious lives economized. True, loss would have been sustained, but to incur slight loss in order to avoid a heavy loss is a process followed every day in trade, and is a very proper business operation.

The garrisons, withdrawn to Portugal and settled in the thinly-populated southern provinces, would have reared families of sturdy soldiery, instead of the debased type that was taking the place of the original stock. These southern provinces had never been completely cultivated, and when the trade with Africa commenced the grandees imported slaves in large numbers. The results are obvious. The slaves worked cheaply or for nothing; the native peasant could not compete with him, and emigrated to Brazil— to the great advantage of Brazil. Moreover, the slave married, and the population thus steadily degenerated. Undoubtedly, the further importation of slaves should have been forbidden, not from moral motives— that could hardly be expected—but from economical and prudential motives. Emigration would have been checked, and the land gradually populated by the returned garrisons from the East.

There was yet another source of strength that was neglected. Brazil was intensely loyal. Throughout all the misfortunes of Portugal not a murmur came from Brazil. The Brazilians were more Portuguese than the Portuguese. This enthusiastic loyalty was entirely neglected by the monarchs of the old country, and yet it asked nothing better than to be granted some share in the service of the empire. It would have been quite in accordance with the spirit of the time to have made grants of land in Brazil, conditional on one son of the family serving a term in the Portuguese army. Some such measure, far from being oppressive, would have been thought a high honour, and would have added another regiment to the home army.

By these and similar measures an armed force of twenty or twenty-five thousand excellent soldiers, trained in the invaluable school of Indian and African warfare, could have been maintained without the slightest inconvenience. That would have sufficed. For what actually happened? Portugal was conquered in the year 1580, and eight years later Spain, her conqueror, was *in extremis*, without a fleet, without money, almost without an army. It was not, therefore, necessary to the preservation of Portugal to keep on foot an army capable of resisting for a generation the whole force of Spain. All that was needed was that there should be such a force in the field as would make

Spain hesitate, or, if she attacked, would hold her occupied and perhaps embarrassed until Spain went to pieces herself. For, besides the direct loss involved in defeat in the field, the Portuguese Empire, as soon as it fell before the Spanish arms, naturally became the prey of all the enemies—and they were many and fierce—of Spain. If Portugal had been fighting Spain, these daring men would have been her enthusiastic allies; and when Drake sailed up the Tagus to 'singe the King of Spain's beard,' instead of burning Portuguese shipping he would have been more likely to land a few hundred brave Englishmen to fight the detested Spaniard side by side with the Portuguese.

There is nothing miraculous in these steps which were not taken; they are simple administrative measures, and could all have been carried out by a royal order. Some vested interests would have been disturbed, but the vested interests were mostly the King's. There was no board of governors to consult or persuade, no body of shareholders to consider, no announcement of falling dividends to be faced. Would Henry the Thinker have hesitated six months over any of them?

The immediate cause of the paralysis of the Portuguese intelligence is to be found in the fact that in the year 1536 the Inquisition was established at Lisbon. It was my fate some years ago, when making an allusion to the work of the Inquisition, to be told, 'There never was any such thing; it is an invention of the Protestants.' It may be so. We have had to give up William Tell, and the Siege of Troy, and very likely it may be before long demonstrated that the Inquisition was only a sun-myth. But if this be established, it may deprive ardent divines of openings for some impassioned periods, but it will redeem the heresies once and for all from the frequent charge of lack of imagination.

In the present state of historical inquiry it appears, however, to be generally accepted that the Inquisition was an important tribunal of the Roman Church, established for the purpose of purifying the faith from errors.

It likewise appears to be established that the principal instrument by which it sought to attain that desirable end was the forcible expulsion, from countries where it was introduced, of all whose opinions deviated from those which were authorized by the Inquisition. Orthodox Jews, of course, were not approved by the Inquisition, neither were those conforming Jews who were called New Christians in Spain and Portugal.

It seems to be established that the disapproval of the Inquisition could not be lightly faced, and in Portugal, in particular, the Jews and New Christians did not attempt to face it at all. Rightly or wrongly they had conceived an unfavourable view of the procedure followed by the Holy Office in cases of heresy or suspected heresy, and they fled in numbers from Lisbon, selling their considerable property at a loss, and often abandoning it altogether.

This behaviour of the Inquisition will appear to be morally reprehensible or not, according to the views of the reader; but socially and economically it was a bad blunder, and in the actual state of Portugal it was a worse disaster than several defeats in the field. But the mischief wrought to Portugal by the establishment of the Inquisition only began with the expulsion of the Jews and New Christians. Disastrous though this was, it was nothing to what followed. The immediate loss was no doubt heavy, including, as it did, loss of men, and a grave shock to credit. But the indirect loss was fatal.

As we have seen, the Portuguese was pre-eminently an agreeable man. His stock had not the force of the Spaniard or the Dutchman, but he was far more human than either. He owed his position largely to his ready sympathy—a truly Christian virtue—with those with whom he dealt, especially with the so-called lower races. He was, at the commencement of the sixteenth century, probably the best type existing. But he possessed no single quality in a transcendent degree. Hence he had need of all his wits if he was to face successfully a Spanish invasion. And it is not too much to say that the Inquisition frightened Portugal out of her wits. Small wonder! But when we remember that it was Thought that founded the Portuguese Empire, we are able to measure, to a certain extent, the damage likely to be wrought by the deliberate paralysis of brain officially brought about by the Sovereign of the country. One is at no small loss to understand the action of the King. The Portuguese were not addicted to heresy. On the contrary, they were faithful and even eager Churchmen, and always did their best towards missionizing the countries they visited or subdued. They did not need a spur for their religious zeal.

We who are accustomed to the sight of a great empire where missionary work not only receives no official sanction, but is rather frowned on than otherwise, must all the more admire the tact of the Portuguese, a tact which enabled them to do all the mighty deeds we know them to have done, while never hesitating to put in the forefront of their schemes the ardent desire to do what most offends Orientals—to proselytize.

What is more, they did proselytize; and they managed to proselytize, not only without getting themselves detested, but in such a way as to add to their influence. No one will contend that the Portuguese Empire was perfect. The civil service, and, for the matter of that, the army, was corrupt, but it was not more corrupt than the civil service of India before Clive took it in hand. There was no irremediably bad feature in their system of administration, and they were cheerful and loyal Churchmen. But the Inquisition ruined them. It scared and demoralized them, and, worst of all, it paralyzed their intellect.

It is almost as great a blunder to ascribe a nation's ruin to a single cause as it is to say that its ruin is 'inevitable,' and although the immediate evil results of the introduction of the Inquisition, and the still more sinister indirect results of the fatal move, seem to justify us in laying a good share of Portugal's ruin to that account, it yet remains to be inquired, 'How came the Inquisition to be introduced?'

It was introduced at the urgent entreaty of the King of Portugal, so that the *causa causans* was the wrongheadedness of the King. If it had not been for the Portuguese Royal Family there would have been no Portuguese Empire—their good qualities founded it, and their bad qualities ruined it. As Portugal was practically a despotism, we may, if we please, say that the downfall of the empire was due to there being no balance of power in the State; so that if accident gave the State an incapable head, there was nothing to hinder him doing his worst.

Still, there have been far worse rulers than John III. and Sebastian (the last two kings before the Captivity, if we omit the Cardinal King, whose reign was very short) whose blunders have not ruined their country. So that we may say, if we please, that the ruin of Portugal was owing to the misfortune which gave her an incompetent King at a critical period.

But this generalization remains : that the foundation and ruin of the Portuguese Empire were the work of the Portuguese

Royal Family. The Portuguese race was not of that toughness of fibre which goes to make a nation of the Imperial mould. It was too gentle and homely. The extraordinary intellectual force of its monarchs did the work of guidance and control, and did it admirably. There was just sufficient imagination in the character of the people to make empire possible; but there was not sufficient stamina to give the empire stability. So long as they had able monarchs, the Portuguese went on from strength to strength; so soon as the royal line grew feeble the empire crumbled to pieces.

As to the future of Portugal, we can judge it best by the past. The future of Portugal is not only, or chiefly, an affair of the people. The people is—as it always was—to a very remarkable degree dependent on the character of its monarchs. To say this is no disparagement. We may say the contrary of Italy and England; but Germany and France—at least equally great nations—are like Portugal in this respect. Though hardly the race they were, the Portuguese have still sufficient vitality to give them character. So lately as the Peninsular War they fought admirably—and fighting is a good test. There is still a Portuguese nation.

But whether there will again be a Portuguese Empire (and this is a question of the greatest importance, not only to Portugal, but to the world) depends on one single consideration, and on one only. France, as we know, having lost one empire, has without delay made for herself another; Spain, as we shall see, possessed the kind of empire that is not to be revived; the empire of Holland persists because, as we shall see, it was restored to her as a free gift. So far of the empires that have in part passed away. It appears that many nations that have not possessed empires in the past are ambitious of founding them in our own days. Some feel themselves driven by overpopulation, and some by what is called destiny, and some (unwillingly) by a menacing will, and some by desire to be in the forefront of modern movement.

None of these controlling forces applied to

Portugal in the past, and we need not seek among them for the force that is to settle her future destiny—whether she is to remain in the list of Imperial Powers, or to subside into a small European State. Thought and the guiding hand of her kings made Portugal great, and the change that has taken place in her fortunes has emphasized the fact that through the genius of her King only can her empire be expected to revive.

III.

THE LOST EMPIRE OF SPAIN.

III.

THE LOST EMPIRE OF SPAIN.

WE are accustomed to congratulate ourselves that the tide of Moslem invasion was rolled back from Spain, and that the Christian kings should have succeeded, after eight hundred years of wars, in expelling Islam from Europe. Our continent was thus saved to civilization, so we are accustomed to reflect; and we place the struggle of Spain against the Moors in the same rank with the struggle of Hellas with Troy, of Rome with Carthage. We feel that in each case the hordes of Asia were thrust back on their native barbarism, and civilization was given time to breathe before the next struggle. Perhaps we are right; but in enduring the yoke of Spain the world paid so fearful a price for its liberation from the sons of Ishmael that there is room for speculation as to whether we should not have been better off if Islam had been permanently encamped in the Peninsula.

Primarily, one would say, this depends on the stamp of ruler that Islam produces. Contemporary with the grand period of the Spanish Empire, Islam produced two very great rulers, Solyman and Akbar. Solyman, one of the greatest of the Turks; and Akbar, not only one of the greatest of the Moguls, but also one of the greatest of the sons of men. Nor has Islam, even in our own days, altogether lost the trick of turning out these grand figures.

Among the men of this century few names deserve to stand higher than that of Sálár Jang. The accident of an early death, and perhaps his religious views, limited his field of influence. But in his mental qualities he ranked with Akbar and Hárún. When Islam produces men like these the world is the better for Muhammadanism. But Islam is not often in labour with men like Sálár

Jang, and it is safer to assume that the Spanish Caliphate would have been ruled by ordinary despots like, for example, Nádir Sháh, or the late Shah Nasr ad Dín. Spain could hardly have been more desolate and disorderly under their control than she was under her own Philips' and Charles'; and Europe would have been saved from those 'conquering bridegrooms' whose alliances threw so fatal a net round her prosperity and happiness. Probably Portugal could not long have maintained her independence, and there would thus have been no Portuguese Empire, which would have been a loss to the world. But there would also have been no Spanish Empire; and that would have been an immeasurable gain.

No people had such great Imperial opportunities as the Spaniards. When the crowns of Castile and Aragon were united, and the Moors were expelled from Spain, the Spaniards found themselves the lords, not only of their own country, but (by the alliances of their kings) the rulers also of Flanders, and of extensive territories in Italy.

Their king became Emperor, and as such held sway over the whole of Central Europe. Soon they became the lords of the New World; yet a century and a half and they had fallen, and their lands were portioned out among aliens.

The Oriental precocity of their development is only one of the many baleful traits that their national character seems to have assimilated during the long strife with Islam.

It is a curious reflection that while intercourse with Islam benefited the Portuguese it damaged the Spaniard. The Portuguese appears to have assimilated from his Saracen antagonists a roaming and adventurous temper, and little else. The Spaniard took on the ponderous gravity of the Turk, and a double portion of his invincible stupidity. It was impossible for him to add to his valour by acquiring the courage of the Mussulman, for no man could be more courageous than the Spaniard of the grand epoch of Spain. It is a marked characteristic of all Oriental or Orientalized peoples that their features fluctuate with the character of their rulers;

and so we saw that the history of Portugal is simply the history of her kings. It is not so with the history of Spain. Either from some strain of independence unconsciously inherited from the days when she had free institutions, or from some other cause, the Spanish nature does not answer readily to the hand of a leader. The Portuguese is flexible enough, if he lacks initiative; but the Spaniard will neither move of his own motive nor follow his leader. In fact, the Spanish mind resembles a street in a Spanish city—lofty, but narrow, with a glimpse of heaven at the top; but rigid and gloomy, and with no invigorating current of outside air to purify its midst.

In Europe her influence was comparatively short-lived. In Holland it was thrown off after appalling horrors had been perpetrated in the vain endeavour to uphold it. In Naples and Sicily, where it persisted, the depressed condition of these two naturally wealthy countries remained a testimony as eloquent of the baleful influence of Spanish government as the condition of Spain itself.

But it is in respect of the New World that civilization brings the heaviest charges against the Spaniards.

In a fine and musical phrase, Mr. Frederick Myers foretells the possible subsidence of the European mind into the 'immemorial sadness of the East.' Perhaps only one can hardly accept that fate as inevitable, or even probable, without a conception of Christian teaching which is far from being universally adopted at present. Besides, there is another alternative. There is the 'immemorial sadness of the East,' but there is also the 'immemorial gaiety of the West.'

We have some reason to look on political success and business capacity as incompatible with gaiety and indiscriminate enjoyment of living. The successful nations of Europe have mostly been the gloomy nations—the Romans, the English. A certain ponderous and haggard devotion to profitable employment is commonly regarded as indispensable to the bearing of an Englishman.

The discovery of the maritime races of the Pacific in various stages of civilization, from the lowest to the highest, who all take such different views of life to our own, and who are capable of becoming our rivals—possibly our successful rivals—in all the graver occupations of life—in war, in trade, in politics; the discovery, in fact, of the immemorial gaiety of the West, will probably end by influencing our views in this respect. Now, if England had fallen on Japan with Maxims and ironclads, and had so handled her that in twenty years' time her arts, her religion, and her whole polity had become nothing but a memory, England would have been responsible for perhaps one-fourth of the damage inflicted on the civilization of the world by the conquests of Spain in the New World. In Mexico, and still more in Peru, mighty material achievements were completed by people who yet carried on life so differently from either Europeans or Asiatics that their civilizations—had they survived—might have taught us lessons of incomparable value. The oft-told story of these two conquests must here be summarized if we would appreciate the Lost Empire of Spain.

'Then felt I like some watcher of the skies
When a new planet swims into his ken;
Or like stout Cortez, when with eagle eyes
He stared at the Pacific, and all his men
Looked at each other with a wild surmise,
Silent, upon a peak in Darien.'

This is the Cortez of imagination. The real Cortez was a practical person, who never made wild surmises about anything; and we know from his own pen that the only reflection that occurred to him on this moving occasion was whether or not the Pacific might prove to be the sea where the reputed pearl islands were, and whether they would be worth looting. That is, as the history of the Spanish Empire reveals to us, the only thing that would occur to a Spaniard, who was the least romantic of mortals. His grave bearing, sonorous mother tongue, and remarkable military achievements, joined, perhaps, to a gloomy picturesqueness in his dress, have combined to give us rather a false impression of the typical hidalgo. They have hidden from us his contented ignorance and his stupid narrowness.

His ferocious intolerance we have good

reason to remember; but we must needs take some pains before we can realize how so vigorous a type may exist, and for a time succeed—may conquer and found an empire —and yet remain destitute of any glimmer of real political capacity, or even of sound business instinct.

Under the guise of a Christian knight, we shall discover a type the nearest approach to which is to be found in a Mussulman emir; and we must offer our apologies to Islam for the comparison.

There would have been no Spanish Empire without Hernando Cortez, who was born in Estremadura in the year 1485. His family were not noble, but they were reputable folk, his father being an officer in the army. Hernando was a youth much addicted to gallantry, and the scrapes that he got into rather scandalized his respectable parents. His last escapade severely lamed him for the time, and prevented him leaving for the New World with the expedition of Ovando.

After all, he began life early, for he was only nineteen years of age when he left

Spain for Hispaniola in the search for gold, without a clear idea of how he was going to get it—much as men leave England now for Buluwayo. He landed, and presented himself at Government House. The Governor was on tour, and Cortez was received by the Private Secretary, who welcomed him with the kindness always shown by private secretaries to young gentlemen on their travels who are properly presented.

Cortez knew Ovando at home, so the secretary was especially polite, and assured him that he would have no difficulty in obtaining a grant of land, and Indians to work it. No doubt he was pleased at the idea of gaining for the colony so promising an immigrant. But Cortez was not excited at the idea of becoming a colonial farmer, and said so. In later years he used to proclaim that his great object was to propagate the Catholic faith, but in youth his motives were more direct. 'I came to get gold,' he said—'and not to till the soil, like a hind,' he added, somewhat ungraciously, we must admit. The secretary was shocked at this unceremonious way of receiving the Governor's favours.

But Cortez's letters of credit were not very heavy; and, after all, a farm as a free gift, with Indian slaves to work it, implied at least a living. The Governor explained to his young friend that gold was not to be picked up every day; so Cortez made the best of his circumstances, and settled down on his land. He led an exciting life, full of love-making and Indian wars, for seven years. It was a life that would have satisfied most men of his temperament; but it did not satisfy Hernando Cortez.

The officer charged by Ovando with the conduct of the numerous wars in Hispaniola was Diego de Velasquez. He had found Cortez a useful man on an expedition, and in the year 1511, when ordered on duty for the conquest of Cuba, his first thought was to secure the young colonist's services. For Cortez it was the choice of Hercules. His estate in Hispaniola was paying well; and he was certain, if he remained in the island, to find himself growing in importance every year, but his dreams of gold would be as far from realization as ever. He accepted Velasquez's offer.

The reduction of Cuba proved to be an easy matter. Velasquez was in high good humour with his lieutenant, and, on being appointed to the Governorship, chose Cortez for Colonial Secretary.

His official position did not, however, bring with it the gravity suitable to his connection with Government House, and he came into collision with the Governor over a love affair in which both men were interested. Velasquez never forgave him; and Cortez found himself in this uncomfortable position—that he had given up a competence in Hispaniola, quarrelled with the Governor of Cuba, and was still as far as ever from realizing his dreams of gold. For want of occupation, he became a conspirator; was detected by the Governor, thrown into prison, and narrowly escaped the gallows. The Governor was now master of the situation. Cortez, having disdained comfort and comparative respectability in his eagerness to acquire a fortune rapidly, found himself with no alternative to passing the rest of his life in gaol, except to do what he was told. He made his peace with the Governor, married the young lady, and settled down as a farmer in Cuba.

There were gold-mines on his estates which could be worked profitably; and Cortez worked them. He became richer than before; but what he was still pining for was a vast fortune, not a mere competence; what he aspired to was the profit of sack and plunder, not the peddling yearly gains of agriculture and trade. Another opportunity for realizing his dreams presented itself in the year 1518. Expeditions had been sent to the mainland by Velasquez, and now returned with the news that there at least gold was quite a common material; men used it for all purposes. Moreover, the land was inhabited by people with a high standard of civilization. The houses were of stone; not of reeds and rushes, as in the islands.

Here evidently was a country well worth plundering; and Cortez, as soon as he heard of it, determined to secure the job for himself. This was not an easy matter; for he was naturally out of favour with the Governor, with whom lay the selection of the captain for the new expedition. He did not make a personal application, but prevailed on those surrounding Velasquez to plead his cause. He was probably the best man that the Governor could find; for, in addition to being a man of proved daring and resource, he had become a substantial person, with means enough to equip the expedition at his own expense. The Governor assented, and Cortez set to work. He succeeded too well, and was too evidently the right man for the work to give entire satisfaction to so suspicious a man as Velasquez.

It was contemplated to revoke his commission, but the friends who had procured it for him gave timely notice of the Governor's intention, and Cortez set sail from Santiago de Cuba without completing his preparations, leaving Velasquez in extreme anger at having been foiled. With massive assurance Cortez, although sailing under the Governor's instructions, in defiance of the Governor's known intention to supersede him, put in at various ports of Cuba, and completed his preparations. Orders were sent to arrest him ; but, under the stimulating influence of an independent command, his character was rapidly developing. He was felt to be a dangerous man to meddle with ; and, making their choice between the displeasure of Velasquez and the displeasure of Cortez, the captains of the various ports where he put in deliberately disobeyed their orders. Cortez completed his preparations at his leisure, and on February 18, 1519, he set sail for the conquest of Mexico. He was thirty-four years of age, and had been fifteen years in the Colonies.

The Aztecs were originally a tribe of North American Indians, who, in the course of their wanderings, settled down on the shores of the Lake of Mexico. About the time of the sixth Crusade, they had just arrived at their Central American home, and built their huts of reeds and rushes on the sunny, sedgy margin of the lake. Thanks to the first

Archbishop of Mexico—who destroyed the State Records in one vast bonfire, conceiving them to be magical instruments!—we know next to nothing of the Aztec history of the next four centuries.

But at the beginning of the sixteenth century the empire of Mexico was a monarchy, hereditary in one family; but the newly-elected Emperor had to prove his capacity before his coronation. The Head of the State might be a person pursuing very ordinary avocations before his call, but his fitness being once demonstrated he received almost divine honours. There was a punctiliously graded aristocracy, and the little Aztec tribe had so multiplied that the land was thickly populated. There was a simple, but efficacious, judicial system, and the judges were independent of the Crown—a state of things not reached in England until a century and a half later. This fact is, by itself, evidence of high political capacity. The military career was honoured, but not more so than trade.

As one consequence of this state of things

—so exceptional in all ages and countries—there was no brigandage. The land, and especially the capital, were carefully policed; the roads were very good. The Aztecs had no beasts of burden, but a busy commerce, nevertheless, covered all the roads with porters; and the Imperial post travelled fast and regularly. One hundred miles in twenty-four hours was the usual time allowed for the transmission of reports. Nor was this pace a characteristic only of the hardy labourers; officers of the Crown were expected to be equally expeditious—and were so. In war or peace the nobles were excellent travellers.

In that intense climate, blazing with sunshine and gorgeous with flowers, it is hardly surprising that the arts flourished. There was no writing except hieroglyphics, little painting, and the music was primitive. It consisted of drum, whistle and conch, and revelled in half-tones and quarter-tones, like the depressing noises that do duty for chants and triumphs in an Indian temple. But, this said, we have reached the limits of Aztec ignorance, and in the other arts they far surpassed Europeans. They were finished goldsmiths. By long practice the art of working in gold seems to have become almost instinctive with them. The Spaniards admitted that Europe had nothing to show that could compare with Mexican goldsmithry. The most delicate specimens were melted down and sent to Spain to pay for the wars of the Emperor—a bitter comment on the Conquest, more eloquent than pages of declamation.

Gold being plentiful, it was used for everything: for decorating armour, for friezes in houses, for table-plate on great occasion—wherever, in fact, it could be employed artistically. The art of decorating in feathers is practically lost. The Mexicans carried it to a high pitch of excellence. Green was the royal colour, but vestments and pálkis were elaborately wrought in the appropriate colours of the owners. Liveries and heraldic devices were of necessity scrupulously observed, as in all feudal States, for much depended on them.

The Aztecs were excellent engineers.

Their capital was built on a lake, and when we consider that the population of Mexico city numbered 300,000, we can form some idea of the amount of causeway and irrigation work necessary to keep order in the midst of so large and busy a population. They were admirable gardeners, cultivating with care, and arranging with the nicest art. The floating gardens on the Lake of Mexico were like fairy creations. It was on these diminutive but exquisite islands that all the market gardening of the capital was done. But many of them were simply floating flower-gardens, created and maintained for the delight of the eye and the pride of life.

In architecture their performances were naturally limited by their ignorance of the use of iron, but they did wonderful things with flint. Their temples were lofty constructions, rising to a height of 100 feet, but the ordinary house was of one or two stories only, and was not remarkable outside; inside it was elegant and light, with suitable and not cumbrous furniture. They were nice in eating and drinking, and were great smokers and snuff-takers. Europe owes to the Aztecs at least one other delicacy—chocolate, which was the favourite drink of the Emperor, and was consequently the only drink for persons of quality. It seems to have been consumed in large quantities, whipped up to the consistency of a very light *bavaroise*, an art which we have lost. The common drink, pulque, still used in Mexico, was slightly intoxicating.

We now come to the astounding fact that a rare and special delicacy at Aztec dinners was human flesh. The God of War was only appropriately worshipped with human sacrifices, and the privilege of consuming flesh thus offered was highly appreciated. The victims were, as a rule, captives taken in battle, and there is no use in blinking the fact that an Aztec temple must have been a hideous spectacle. The frightful effigy of the god looked down on an altar, only rightly served when it bore a human heart. The walls were foul with the splashes of stale blood, and the priests were the only people in Mexico whom we can rightly call savages. Their ritual was loathsome, but their prayers (of which some have fortunately been preserved) were lofty and dignified. As transliterated into English, the Mexican tongues appear to be hideous jargon, but the Europeans who first heard them spoken described them as both sonorous and elegant. It was not written, but the Mexicans had elaborated the art of picture-writing, at which they had grown adepts. The State papers were kept in a sort of record-office. As has been mentioned, Zumarraga, the first Archbishop of Mexico, destroyed all that he could lay his hands on.

The great blot on the national life was the habit of human sacrifice. It was no doubt as debasing to the national character as the bull-fights of the Spaniards ; more so, perhaps. When all is said, it was shocking to the last degree, but it was a habit pursued by our own ancestors a few centuries earlier. It disappeared from England under the influence of milder teaching. In the modified degree of Satí it was practised in India not so long since, and was suppressed by a simple legislative enactment. No doubt the Aztecs who had raised themselves so high in four short centuries would have dropped the habit in time. It had already been practically suppressed in the neighbouring and federated State of Tezcuco.

If we seek for a parallel to aid our conception of the Aztec State, we shall find it in Japan. In both countries we find the same religious reverence for the Emperor, the same punctiliously-graded aristocracy, the same instinctively artistic peasantry, the same capacity for political work, the same fierce and dauntless spirit in war. The Aztecs were behindhand in that their religion was gloomy and bloody, but the Japanese lagged behind the Aztecs in the extravagant prominence that they awarded to the military caste.

Such was the mighty and wealthy State that Cortez proposed to subdue with an army of 863 men, all told, of whom 200 were Indians. On April 21, 1519, he landed on the site of the city of Vera Cruz, and for the first time realized the difficulties of his vast enterprise. Although he was never turned aside from his determination to conquer Mexico, either by the mutiny of his followers or the loss of battles, he felt for long after the outset an intense anxiety as to the means he should employ to that stupendous end.

It was cheering to observe the terror with which the natives regarded his cavalry. Having never seen a horse and his rider before, they regarded them as supernatural beings. This was to the good, but he only had sixteen horses. He was fortunate in obtaining two interpreters, one a Spaniard, the survivor of an earlier expedition, the other a beautiful Indian girl, who never forsook him throughout all his trials and dangers. Through them he learnt something of the politics of Central America, and he turned his information to his use with a dexterity and courage truly Napoleonic. He very soon heard the name of Montezuma, the reigning Emperor, and it became plain that there were rifts within the fabric of the Aztec

State, which, if widened, might well bring it to the ground.

Montezuma had been on the throne for seventeen years when Cortez landed, and had made his name a terror through all the borders of Anahuac. He was a successful soldier, but his early training had been for the priesthood. He was intensely orthodox, and regarded the proper supply of human victims as one of his first duties. His wise old uncle, the King of Tezcuco, had nearly succeeded in stamping out human sacrifices, but Montezuma was not a reformer, any more than Philip II. Like the Spanish King, he loved seclusion, and took a Satanic pride in his rank. He loved to isolate himself in semi-divine solitude; his sole pleasure was in making other men obey him—if possible, obey him unwillingly. We must be content therefore, in spite of his misfortunes, to rank him with the second-rate men. If he had, during the seventeen years of his reign, shown the slightest desire to conciliate, the Spaniards might have found on their landing a united nation that would have driven them back to their ships. Montezuma was powerful; he would be omnipotent—and he fell.

For there were those within the boundaries of the Aztec Empire who would not obey the Emperor. At their head were the men of Tlascala, a republican State on the Atlantic border of Mexico. The Tlascalans were the Swiss of Central America. They had repulsed the Aztecs over and over again, and maintained their independence in spite of menaces and offers. The power of Montezuma was so great that he was able to cause them very great discomfort by cutting them off from food supplies. They lived hardly, but were stubbornly determined to maintain their independence. The Emperor had treated them with particular cruelty, and at the time when Cortez landed they had a frenzied hatred for the city of Mexico and its monarch, a hatred that (as we shall see) closed their ears to all appeals of reason or self-interest.

All this was explained to Cortez soon after his landing, and he listened attentively, with outward indifference, but intense inward gratification. If he could win over the Tlascalans, his conquest was assured, and he was the more resolved to persist in his endeavours when he heard of a certain legend that was current throughout the domains of Montezuma. This was the legend of the fair god who had sailed away into the East, and had promised to return in the fulness of time, when the Aztec dominion was to come to an end. Was Cortez the fair god? all men eagerly inquired, and Cortez replied that he was.

This judicious assumption of the Divine character had far wider and deeper results than Cortez could have anticipated at the time. For Montezuma was learned in all the lore of his religion, and was perfectly acquainted with the legend of the fair god. He knew that the time was near when, according to prophecy, he should return and claim his own, and, being a very religious man, he hardly dreamed of opposing the Divine invader. Thus the resistance of the city of Mexico was paralyzed from the outset—a most important point, for the

Mexicans were quite as good fighters as the Tlascalans, and were better armed and provided, besides being more numerous. So, fighting where necessary, diplomatizing wherever possible, Cortez slowly made his way through Zempoalla, Tlascala and Cholula, and on November 8, 1519, he made his formal entry into the fairy city of Mexico.

The Emperor had done all that lay in his power, short of fighting, to delay the march of the Spaniards. He had sent embassy after embassy, each laden with presents more magnificent than the last, and all conveying the regret of Montezuma that he could not receive Cortez in his capital. But Cortez was not the man to be put aside with polite phrases, and his repeated assurances that the message he bore from his master could only be delivered to the Emperor in his capital were telling on the superstitious mind of Montezuma. The mere expression of the despot's wish had been, until the arrival of the Spaniards, enough to awe all men into acquiescence; and here were men who not only declined to obey him, but were resolved on taking precisely the opposite course to that which he hinted was the proper one. Moreover, besides the presumption from prophecy that the strangers were divine, there was other and very tangible evidence of the fact. The Emperor had seen Cortez take the road that led through Tlascala with great satisfaction; for he hoped that in this mountainous region the Spaniards would be destroyed. In the recesses of his mind there was still a lingering hope that, after all, Cortez might not be the divine being that he pretended to be, and he trusted that the Tlascalans would settle the question for him.

There was great debate in the Tlascalan Senate as to the course the Republic should take, and the first decision had been for war. Deep was the consternation of Montezuma, when his couriers brought him the news that Cortez had made mincemeat of the Republicans. His musketry, his mail-clad warriors, and his dreaded cavalry, had cut their finest armies to pieces; and his own diplomacy had subsequently converted the foes of Montezuma into the allies of the Spaniards. Thus the men who entered Mexico now came, not only as mysterious strangers, but accompanied by 6,000 Tlascalan guards, who followed them like well-trained dogs who knew their master.

With grand courtesy the Emperor came out to meet the dreaded strangers. He welcomed them to his capital, and assigned a vast palace for their residence, sufficiently spacious to accommodate not only the Spaniards, but also the whole of the Tlascalan auxiliaries. It was with some trepidation and infinite precaution that Cortez established himself in his new quarters. In this city of solid buildings, interlaced with deep canals, and swarming with a warlike and unfriendly population, there was every chance that he might be cut off, and overwhelmed by mere force of numbers. An exchange of visits followed, during one of which Montezuma owned the supremacy of the Spanish Crown, probably not very clearly understanding what he was doing. But Cortez was more discouraged than ever when he had seen the Emperor's court and capital. The busy markets, perfectly ordered, where on booths smothered in gorgeous flowers all the products of a continent were displayed for sale, gave a most depressing idea of the resources of the Aztec State.

As for the Court, the long lines of bowing nobles, the gorgeous ceremonials, the incense rising everywhere, the etiquette more rigid and more punctiliously exacted than the etiquette of Spain itself, the unparalleled beauty of the interior of the palace, left but one impression on the conquistadores. They were now, indeed, in the lions' den. They durst not, even if they had an excuse, attack an empire of such strength ; yet, if they did not, nothing remained but to retreat to Cuba, where they would be covered with ignominy for their failure, and probably be brought to trial by Velasquez. If they merely stayed on as guests in the city of Mexico, they would not be advancing their cause, even if they were not superseded by a fresh expedition sent from Cuba, or from Spain itself. They were desperate men, and none was more desperate than their chief. He called to his aid the same sublime assurance with which, as a lad of nineteen, he told the Governor of Hispaniola that he wanted gold, not lands— with which he had provisioned his expedition in the ports of Cuba against the express orders of the Governor. He kidnapped the Emperor, and put him in chains in the Spanish quarters. The chains were soon removed, but Montezuma remained a prisoner. Fifteen hundred thousand pounds sterling were exacted from him under the name of a present to the King of Spain, to whom he formally swore allegiance.

Cortez, having obtained an advantage, pressed it home, and the Emperor sank to the position of a puppet in the Spaniard's hands. The people were wild with rage and consternation; but the Emperor (to save his own pride) repeatedly assured them that he was there of his own will; so all excuse for rising was taken away. Nevertheless, a rising appeared imminent, and at the same time the alarming news was brought to

Cortez that a new expedition had landed at Vera Cruz, with orders to bring him to trial for disobedience to the instructions of Velasquez.

The latter news was much more disquieting than the discontent of the Aztecs. It was another crisis in the fate of Cortez. Leaving behind him as many men as he could afford to spare, he marched against his new enemies. Narvaez was in command, an incompetent vapouring soldier, who could not be roused into vigilance even by the news, which reached him on all hands, of Cortez' astonishing achievements. Had he been a man of ordinary capacity, even of such humble military capacity as consists in keeping a watch at night, Cortez' days had been numbered; for Narvaez' forces were numerically far stronger than the little band of conquistadores. However, a night surprise gave Cortez the victory, with very little bloodshed, and diplomacy completed his triumph the next day. He represented to Narvaez' men how much more profitable it would be to share in the plunder of Mexico than to go back to Cuba on the pay of a common soldier, and the result was that he marched back to the city of Mexico much stronger than when he had started.

Alvarado, who had stayed behind to guard Montezuma, was a savage man, who could think of no better way of stilling the Aztec discontent than to entrap 600 of the nobles in an enclosed courtyard and slaughter them. This act precipitated the rising of the people, and immediately on Cortez' return it broke out. The Spaniards were besieged in their quarters. It was an additional misfortune for them that the captive Emperor was mortally wounded by the hands of his own subjects as he was endeavouring to quiet them. The Spaniards thus lost what was a perpetual guarantee for their safety and indemnity for their conduct. All hope was now gone; the worst had happened, and nothing remained but for Cortez to cut his way out as best he could. He contrived to do so, but only with the loss of all his guns, most of his treasure, and half his men. His Tlascalan allies were hewn down by the hundred, and he himself was severely wounded. More than half the Spaniards, and more than two-thirds of the Tlascalans, were killed—about 4,450 all told—in the disastrous night-retreat known to history as the Triste Noche, July 1, 1520. Cortez had to fight one more great battle in the open; and at last, half dead himself, and with a band of followers who hardly looked like an armed force, he found shelter within the hospitable walls of Tlascala.

The Aztecs now gave proof of high political capacity. They sent messengers to Tlascala, saying: 'We grant that we have behaved badly to you in the past; but consider how much more dangerous are these white men to the peace of our country than any excesses of tyranny on our part can be—excesses that we promise shall not be repeated in the future. As for these white men, we received them kindly, and see what they have done; they have profaned our temples and plundered our treasure; they led our Emperor captive, and he died in their hands. Our sons have died by the thousand to expel them from our city of Mexico. You see, they are not gods, as they pretended, but mortals like ourselves, only better armed. If we have been faithless in the past, the white men are still more perfidious. You see how they treated us, even so will they treat you. But join us now in expelling them before more come, and we will arrange our differences among ourselves.'

The fate of Central America trembled in the balance. It was the older men, reputed wise, who were in favour of Cortez; the young men, of whom the chief was shortly after hanged by Cortez, reputed rash, showed the greater foresight. The elders said: 'Let us break Mexico, and we will then deal with Cortez'; the younger said: 'Nay, we know that we can at least hold our own against Mexico, but these terrible strangers have beaten us all over and over again, and we know not what they may do. They are now in our power; let us make an end of them.' Age and authority and the traditions of prescriptive policy carried the day, and the embassy of the Aztecs returned after a parting jeremiad over the impending fate of Anahuac.

At his leisure, and in the secure ease assured to him by the credulous Tlascalans, Cortez soon recovered from his wounds, and prepared for his final campaign. He built twelve brigantines, with which to operate on the Lake of Mexico, and had them carried on the shoulders of porters to the shores of the Lake. He raised levies, supplemented by the fortunate arrival of a reinforcement of men and horses from the islands, and at last, with 100,000 auxiliaries and 900 Spaniards, he stood once more before the city of Mexico.

Under the leadership of their young Emperor, Guatemozin, the successor of Montezuma, the Aztecs fought like tigers. They cut their dykes, like the Hollanders, and disputed every inch of the way into their beloved capital. They repulsed many assaults, on one occasion capturing sixty-two Spaniards, who were sacrificed alive in batches under the eyes of their comrades in the camp of the besiegers. At one time it seemed as if the allies would have melted away before the tremendous labours of reducing the Aztec capital, and without his allies Cortez could have done but little. But the genius of their commander carried the day. Famine did most of the work, and, after a three months' siege, Cortez entered the heap of ruins that stood where, eighteen months before, the city of Mexico had shone, a fairy creation, and the conquest of Mexico was complete. About 50,000 of the victors had perished during the long blockade; 120,000 Aztec corpses, at the lowest computation, choked the streets and canals of the ruined capital. The Emperor was captured, and received assurance of Cortez' great regard for his indomitable courage. He was assured that a Spaniard knew how to respect a chivalrous enemy.

'They praised him to his face with their courtly foreign grace.'

He was then tortured, in order to make him reveal the whereabouts of the Aztec treasure, and was shortly after strung up by the roadside like a detected footpad. Mexico, as a civilized State, disappeared from the face of the earth, and its place was taken by a bastard Spain, whose sordid barbarism was so long a blot on the face of the earth.

This is, in a few words, the net result of Spanish interference in the New World—the substitution of barbarism for civilization. It was a retrograde movement of a violent, even a cataclysmic, nature. A whole chapter of the world's history was blotted out—a vivid and picturesque type of humanity was destroyed, and the world is not advantaged by the inferior type that has taken its place. This is the grand contrast between the work of England and the work of Spain. The former is creative and conservative, the latter was destructive.

It is no doubt possible to cavil at the work of England, but these facts remain: That the Spaniard destroyed records where the Englishman laboriously collects and preserves them; the Spaniard ruthlessly stamped out Paganism where England has punctiliously and jealously abstained from any official interference whatever with the faith of her non-Christian subjects. Spain blotted out old arts and crafts, and destroyed monuments of quaint learning by the cartload. England carefully and even tenderly preserves the mosques and temples of India, even where the failing means, and perhaps the waning faith, of their votaries throw on her a task that, from no narrow point of view, is no part of her duty.

It may be that England will find her account hereafter a heavy one; it may be that she is earning for herself the denunciation of the Laodiceans. Such is not the opinion of the present writer, and, indeed, it can hardly be the opinion of anyone except a religious fanatic. Let us, however, admit that to be the case; let us grant that the horrible tale of destruction that goes by the name of the Conquest of the New World has laid up for Spain a crown of glory, in that she has made a vast population Christian.

There remains the less transcendental view of the duties of a governing State, and if we consider merely which of the two has contributed to the sum of human happiness and which has diminished it, we need not mind being convicted of error, and perhaps worse than error, so long as in the broad outlines of our policy we have contrived to differ *toto cœlo* from the policy of Spain.

Just three centuries after the downfall of Mexico the country threw off the yoke of Spain, and, after some natural turbulence, has, in the last twenty years, raised itself once more to the rank of a respectable State. Side by side with the destruction of Spanish influence, a sensible diminution in the infusion of Spanish blood has gone on. Native blood has asserted itself, and, under the guise of a Christian Republic, we are now face to face with what is practically a new Aztec State.

The Conquest of Mexico is generally discussed as if it were a question of the personal merits or demerits of Hernando Cortez. By birth he was a gentleman, and upon occasion he behaved like a gentleman, but he was quite prepared to behave like a ruffian if occasion demanded it; he had no prejudices. He was created a marquis by his grateful sovereign. On the death of his first wife he married a duke's daughter, and lived in great magnificence.

The Conquest of Mexico is illumined by the glamour which always gathers round the exploits of a young man; but the Conquest of Peru has missed that attraction. Cortez was a man of decent birth, some slight education, and no small official experience. But the conquerors of Peru were little better than beach-combers. Francis Pizarro was a colonial desperado. He was one of the most illustrious of the illustrious race of bastards—like another conquistador, William of Normandy. He was an ignorant man, and could neither read nor write. At an early age he left his native country, and is first heard of in 'the islands' at the age of thirty-nine. By this expression we mean nowadays the South Sea Islands, but in Pizarro's time it meant the West Indies.

Here, so report went, a man might make his way, even if he had no father to speak of. If he failed, there was always sport to console him—sport of the kind dear to a Spaniard's heart, hunting natives with bloodhounds and similar diversions. At any rate, it was better than herding swine, which was all he had to look forward to in the old country. It would seem as if Pizarro was the very man to succeed in a lawless country like this. He had a frame of iron, an expression often misused, but not out of place here, when we consider the miraculous feats of endurance that he performed in Peru. He was devoid of any of the softer impulses of mankind : he had no fear, no pity, no shame, and no faith—except the Catholic faith. Such a man ought to succeed anywhere, and especially in the rough life of the islands.

But Pizarro had no luck. Youth passed away, and middle-age came and was some way advanced, and still Pizarro was knocking about the islands, leading a lawless and adventurous life, but without regular employment, without money, and without credit. Youngsters who might have been his sons were making names and fortunes, but Pizarro, who was grizzled now, was a beachcomber still, nameless, unsuccessful, poor, discredited, and fifty years of age.

Then came the Conquest of Mexico, and Pizarro, who, had the expression been invented, would have said that the islands were 'played out,' felt that it was time to move on ; so he sailed to Mexico.

But nothing much came of it. The fighting was over, the spoil apportioned, and the country was fast assuming a settled aspect, with officials who frowned on fresh adventurers. So Pizarro drifted across the country to Panama, a city which shares with Múltán the reputation of being separated from the lower regions only by a sheet of paper. Panama was the extremest point of the Spanish dominions, and officialdom had not yet got it into order. It bore the reputation that Callao does to-day, and Pizarro was at home in its congenial atmosphere.

Moreover, there were rumours abroad of a new Mexico, as yet undiscovered, and lying to the south. One or two expeditions had been fitted out, but had returned empty-handed, and brought news of a barren coast and frightful storms encountered at sea. But they also brought the news that every

Indian they had spoken to had persisted in the story of a great country as rich in gold as Mexico, that did indubitably exist, and apparently asked nothing better than to be conquered. This was good enough for Pizarro, who asked nothing better than to be a conquistador. The difficulty, of course, was money. The desperadoes of Panama might be persuaded to volunteer for the expedition on the chance of plunder, although even that much was not positively certain, as the chance seemed remote. But for the purchase or hire of a ship, and for its provisioning with stores and arms, a considerable sum was needed.

The Governor would do nothing for the expedition; he did not believe in the Eldorado, and he did not care about Pizarro. The *deus ex machina* was the Vicar of Panama, who came forward and supplied the necessary funds for Pizarro and his fellow bastard adventurers. It subsequently transpired that he was acting for the Licentiate Espinosa, who really found the money.

However, the Vicar was a respectable

person—the only respectable man of the three, in fact—and the money that he produced and the support of his name were invaluable to the adventurers, Pizarro and Almagro. Two little ships were found and provisioned, and manned with about 100 desperadoes, led and commanded by the most desperate of them all — Francisco Pizarro. Almagro stayed behind to complete the furnishing of the second vessel, and Pizarro set sail alone in November, 1524; he was fifty-three years of age.

We must not confuse the expedition of Pizarro down the western coast of America with the expedition of the Portuguese down the coast of Africa a century earlier. Pizarro was not anxious to add to the sum of human knowledge; he was not interested in new civilization. He had no desire to trade, or to see new countries for the sake of experience. His one object was gold, and he intended to get gold by looting. The hardships that he sustained during the next seven years were almost miraculously supported by himself and his followers; but to describe his expedition as 'chivalrous' or 'crusading' would be to forget altogether the proper use of those words. For Pizarro it was neck or nothing; the chance of a miserable death on the one hand, and the certainty of a prison in Panama on the other. To persist was to face almost unendurable hardships, but to turn back was to end his days in gaol amid the derision of the colony of Panama.

It would be ridiculous not to allow Pizarro the fullest praise—and no praise can be too great—for his endurance and resolution; these were so great that it is inexplicable that he should have passed so many years in poverty and comparative insignificance. But it is surely no less ridiculous to exalt him into a knight-errant, a crusader, and a missionary. He was a desperate gambler, playing with borrowed money, and staking on numbers.

The extraordinary struggle with adverse fortune lasted for seven years. Pizarro and his men sailed through fearful storms, and landed on the shore of what is now Ecuador. They waded through swamps — tropical swamps—some died of fever, some from alligators and snakes, and some from starvation. The survivors subsisted, like marooned sailors, on berries and shell-fish. They cast themselves away on a desert island so as to be free to breathe for a while air that was not actually pestilential.

After two years of separate wandering, Pizarro and Almagro met, half-naked and half-starved. Pizarro had not done much, but Almagro had collected some gold and silver ornaments, and both had collected information as to the existence of Peru, so definite that it was quite plain that a better-found expedition would have no difficulty in reaching the land of gold. Two things they had learnt: they must not start in the rainy season, and they must not waste their strength in the swampy coast-country, but sail further south, where there was drier land and more open roads. But money was wanted for this, so to Panama they must needs repair.

The Governor was furious with them. In his eyes they were pestilent fellows. He did not want to hear about the new countries they had discovered—what Spaniard would? He did not praise them for their endurance; he only cursed them for losing lives that might have been of some use to him. If he could have thrown them into gaol he would gladly have done so. Never was man less adventurously minded than the Governor of Panama.

But Pizarro and his friend met with sympathizers in the colony. Although they had not brought back a fortune, they had brought back something; they were no longer penniless. And once more the Vicar came to the rescue. He advanced 20,000 pieces of eight on the condition that the spoils of Peru should be divided equally between himself and the two adventurers. He administered the Holy Eucharist to them over the bargain, and the congregation was melted to tears as he divided the consecrated wafer into three portions, symbolical of the threefold partition of Peru. It is difficult to see what there was to weep over, and the tears, unless they were prophetic of the fate of the Inca, were misplaced. The Governor was so far softened by the appearance of a cash basis for the operations that he gave the expedition his goodwill. What the value of the Governor's goodwill might be is not quite clear. Probably it amounted to this, that the adventurers were to be unmolested by the officials of the port. The Governor's price was moderate—1,000 pieces of eight—and the adventurers gladly paid it out of the Vicar's loan.

The colonists of Panama seem to have been easily cast down. When all was said and done, Pizarro's losses had not been very heavy. On his first voyage he had started out with 200 men, of whom, after two years' wandering in the most unwholesome climate in the world, he had nevertheless contrived to bring back 150. But this mortality was quite enough to dissuade the men of Panama, desperate though they were, from trying their luck with him, and it was chiefly from a band of immigrant adventurers that he enlisted his crews for the second venture. They made a more open country and tried to penetrate inland, but the natives had grown wary: they armed and drove the Spaniards back to their ships. It was out of the question to try the country they had been baffled in before, and Pizarro accordingly retreated to the island of Gallo in about N. Lat. 2°, and sent Almagro to Panama to ask for more help.

Why he did not proceed south is not quite evident; probably his crews would not have permitted the venture. They wanted large profits and quick returns, and had no stomach for discovery for discovery's sake. So Pizarro laid up at Gallo, and Almagro went to Panama to ply the Vicar and the new Governor.

The Vicar stood to his guns, but the Governor was determined to put up with no more nonsense. He despatched a vessel to Gallo with orders to bring away every Spaniard that was left alive, and to put an end, once and for all, to Pizarro's ridiculous and costly filibustering schemes. The ship arrived, and the officer in command announced his instructions. Pizarro refused to obey them, and thirteen of his fellows stood by him; the rest returned to Panama in the Governor's ship.

It was the policy of the suspicious Government of Spain to allow no Governor to hold his post long enough to gain any local influence, and Pedrarias was by now replaced by a new Governor. We have seen what his temper was, but the Vicar knew of a weak point in the new Governor's armour. It seems that he had, in point of fact, been commanded by the Council of the Indies (or, as we should call it, the Colonial Office) to give Pizarro what help he wanted. So, by working judiciously on this clause, it was finally wrung from the Governor as an act of grace that a Spanish vessel should be placed at Pizarro's disposal for six months, at the expiration of which period he was positively commanded to return to Panama and report progress.

He was absent, not six months, but eighteen, and when he re-appeared, he had long been given up for dead by the entire colony. During his long absence he had discovered the Empire of the Incas. He applied to the Governor for funds to help him to subjugate and plunder it, and was met with a flat refusal. It was not that the Governor had any humane scruples. He merely looked on Pizarro's application as an unsound business-offer, which he had no intention of accepting, or even of furthering in any way. The adventurers were in despair. Once more the Vicar came to the rescue, raised funds to enable Pizarro to cross the seas and lay his plans before the Emperor, and despatched him to Spain with his blessing. On his arrival he was arrested and thrown into prison for an old debt. But the Emperor soon put a stop to this summary process.

Charles was a Fleming, or a Burgundian, rather than a Spaniard; and he was not popular in Spain. Spain to the Spaniard was the only country in the world, but to Charles it was only one of his many provinces. He was not at home with the Spaniards; he did not like their pride, which he thought ridiculous, or their quarrelsomeness, which fretted his own diplomatic temper. They bored him to death, and he was happiest when away from their pretentiousness, and their spiteful and intriguing politics. But he was a good business-man, and did not neglect details. The Colonial enterprises of Spain he had conducted from the outset so as to guard his own pocket, and had given them no other attention, until the success of Cortez had showed him that it was worth his while to do so. His quick insight taught him that in Pizarro he had found another adventurer, who, if carefully managed, would fill his pockets with gold at no expense to himself. He had no intention of losing so favourable an opportunity. So Pizarro was set at liberty and sent for to Toledo.

In their ways of doing business the Spaniards were, as they are, Orientals. We find everywhere the same personal jealousies and intrigues that hinder affairs in an Eastern Court. Nothing moves with the regularity of the affairs of a great State; backstairs rule prevails everywhere. Not even the favour of the Sovereign exempts a man from the necessity of paying *bakhshish*. And all this, not in periods of a nation's decay as in Spain at present, or in England under Charles II., but in the full tide of national prosperity, and at a time when their King was a man of the highest capacity, and was Emperor as well as King.

Pizarro found this out soon enough. His thrifty monarch had dignified him with high-sounding titles, and a new coat of arms, had commanded him to conquer and tranquillize Peru, and had been graciously pleased to command Pizarro to transmit to him one-fifth of the plunder. But he had neglected to supply him with the means to equip his fleet. However, he got it together somehow. The Colonial Office made a last bid for *bakhshish*, and announced their intention of inspecting his vessels, to see if their regulations had been complied with. Pizarro knew what that meant, so he started immediately, and in January, 1530, sailed for the New World.

As a conquistador, Pizarro showed himself a capable pupil of Cortez ; but it must be admitted that he had a much easier task to perform. The Peruvians were as far above the Aztecs as the Aztecs were above the Spaniards. In the first voyage of Pizarro to Peru, they had welcomed him and his men with the enchanting gaiety and hospitality of the better tribes of the South Seas, but they were far more advanced than any of those agreeable people. The externals of life were the same—flowers and dance and song and graceful manners—but the Peruvians had worked out for themselves a civilization so exalted and so beautiful that of the twin destroyers, Cortez and Pizarro, to whom the world owes an undying grudge, Pizarro must take the first place.

The Peruvian State included practically the whole of the West of South America. Englishmen mostly test civilization by material achievements; so perhaps the greatest claim that the Incas have to our respect will be found in the fact that the whole of this difficult country, traversed by giant ranges of mountains, was crossed by roads which were miracles of engineering skill. They were kept in excellent order, and, like those of Mexico, were quite free from the hordes of brigands who swarmed over the roads in Europe, to the disgrace of our government, for centuries after the downfall of the Incas.

The Peruvians were not a trading people; their tastes were pastoral. Their system of government was socialistic, every family being an object of State care. Their religion was simple—sun-worship. The Emperor was not only the head of their civil polity, and their leader in war, but was himself revered as a Child of the Sun. They were a much milder race than the Aztecs; simpler, gayer, and at once less ceremonious and more sociable. The abundance of gold and silver and emeralds gave all their entertainments a sumptuousness that was quite in keeping with their brilliant climate and their beautiful houses. If a chief object of government be to increase the happiness of the governed, never was government so meritorious or so successful as that of the Incas.

The force with which Pizarro proposed to subvert this happy State consisted of 177 men, of whom 67 were cavalry. He landed, and announced, like Cortez, his intention of visiting the Inca in his camp. There was no need to fight his way, for the Peruvians welcomed him everywhere with kindness and hospitality. The reigning Emperor's name was Atahuallpa. He seems to have been devoid of any tincture of Montezuma's suspiciousness, and felt himself far too grand a monarch to regard the strangers as anything but interesting visitors. Pizarro was very uneasy as to the possible results of his temerity. So far as he had gone his schemes had excited no enthusiasm, and his men followed him uninterestedly, murmuring every now and then at the long time it took them to find gold. Every day, as the Spaniards advanced into the heart of the Inca's dominions, and witnessed the ordered strength of the Government, their leader felt more and more certain that only by a bold stroke, like that of Cortez, could he hope to gain any footing. Allies were not to be had ; alone they must achieve whatever they were going to do—277 Spaniards against an empire!

They found the Emperor at last at Caxamalca. He was a stately person, of very noble presence, thirty years of age, with an air of unchallenged authority. His Court was gorgeous; and his retinue, unlike the somewhat ragged bands of followers who crowd round an Eastern Monarch, not only resplendent, but orderly. He was concluding a campaign; and the feudal levies—very numerous levies—were assembled round his camp.

The Emperor was evidently not much impressed by the Spaniards. He was distantly polite, and promised to return their visit. He did not load them with costly presents, or show any anxiety lest they might be supernatural beings. At this rate, the Spaniards would not find their adventure very profitable. When the Emperor had returned their visit they would have no reason for staying any longer in the country. They were greatly cast down. Pizzaro felt that it was now or never. He left the square in which the Inca was to be received empty, posting his men, armed to the teeth, in the corridors of the stone buildings surrounding the square.

After some delay, the Inca arrived, borne in a litter of solid gold, and surrounded by a bodyguard of unarmed nobles and a considerable train of followers. The square was empty, and the Inca halted, and inquired, with pardonable displeasure, where the strangers might be. Father Valverde, the chaplain of the expedition, acted the somewhat undignified part of decoy. He stepped forward, and delivered a long sermon, commencing with the fall of man, and concluding with the direct episcopal authority of the Pope.

Considering the relative position of the two men, there is something grandly courteous in the scene: the omnipotent, divinely-descended Emperor patiently listening to a crazy harangue instead of receiving the stately expressions of welcome and deference to which he had been accustomed all his life.

When Father Valverde arrived at the point of his argument which was concerned with the Pope giving Peru to Charles V., it is not to be wondered at that the Inca's temper gave way. It was his death-signal. At the priest's exhortation, and promise of absolution — this was apparently important — the Spaniards rushed from their ambush, and the slaughter commenced. The Peruvians, of course, had no chance; nor had the Inca. How many thousands fell is uncertain, and not very important; the rest fled, and the Inca remained a prisoner in Pizaro's hands.

In Pizarro's hands he received the attention due to a sovereign : was allowed to hold his Court, and to receive his officers, and give orders relative to the administration of his dominions. The Spaniards were amazed at the deference shown to a man in the Inca's forlorn position by nobles of the highest distinction and authority. They grew more uneasy than ever. It was plain that they had to deal with a very remarkable man.

The days slipped by, and their position grew anxious. They had to mount guard day and night, and, though it might be an important post to mount guard over a reigning sovereign, it put no money into their pockets.

It was some time before Atahuallpa quite realized what the Spaniards really were after. Father Valverde exhorted him constantly to be christened, alleging that the propagation of the true faith was the only object the Spaniards had in hand. His dissertations seem to have interested the Inca, but he found a difficulty in reconciling their tenour with the forcible kidnapping and imprisonment of himself and the murder of his subjects. It was perhaps natural that a man who, all his life, had made no more account of gold than of string should take some time to realize what avarice meant. However, he found out at last, and offered Pizarro a ransom. He undertook to fill his cell with gold up to a certain height. The notary was directed to record the offer with the measurements of the apartment—the Spaniards were careful men of business!

Pizarro did not believe the Inca: nevertheless, the magic of the Sovereign's name brought gold pouring into Caxamalca. The treasury was emptied, the palaces stripped, the temples despoiled; and long before the allotted sum had been realized the Spaniards' mouths were watering with the lust of gain. They loudly clamoured for a division of the spoil; their leader assented. The royal fifth was set aside; and, after infinite squabblings and reproaches, the division was effected. Each foot-soldier got ten thousand pounds; each horse-soldier twice as much. Pizarro took the Inca's golden litter and about a hundred and fifty thousand pounds. The lowest estimate of the total ransom is three millions and a half sterling.

The conquest of Peru being Pizarro's object, the first part of his plan was, of course, to reward his men, and keep them in a good temper. That was attained: his ruffians were in excellent cue. The next step was to get rid of the Inca. If they set him at liberty, it was clear, from what they had seen of his bearing in prison, that he would speedily regain his power, and the Spaniards would have to retreat.

The Inca therefore must die. There

were many ways by which this might be accomplished—poison, drowning, cold steel, or, best of all, an attempt at escape, or a rescue followed by an accident. But none of these simple and commonplace methods were to Pizarro's taste. Like a true Spaniard, he loved the pomp and circumstance of crime; and in the case of the murder of Atahuallpa he was able to indulge his taste. He determined to bring the Inca to trial.

The high court of justice that sat for the trial of the lord of Peru consisted of Pizarro and Almagro. There was, of course, no charge that could possibly be brought against the prisoner, but the court made out a list of four crimes: firstly, his usurpation of the crown; secondly, his lavishing of the treasures of Peru on his own friends and relations; thirdly, his practice of idolatry; and, fourthly, inciting rebellion against the Spaniards. There was one point—the last—on which there might have been some evidence to collect, and, in point of fact, the Spaniards had already tried to collect some. But the trial and condemnation was completed without troubling about evidence, and, as a matter of fact, there was none. If it is worth while to distinguish one charge from the others, the second is perhaps the masterpiece, considering that the only lavishing of treasure that had taken place was the plunder of the treasury for the benefit of the judges. Father Valverde was deferred to as to whether it was right to execute the judgment, and gave it as his opinion that the Inca deserved to die. He was condemned to be burnt to death.

The time chosen was two hours after sunset. The great square of Caxamalca was dark; but by the starlight men could see in the centre a darker spot than the surrounding earth: it was the pile of faggots. Slowly the Spaniards filed in and took their places round the sides of the square; they bore torches. When the glare grew steady, Father Valverde emerged, addressing Atahuallpa, who followed in chains. He was laid on the pile. Up to this moment the Inca had rejected Christianity, saying that he would die in the faith of his fathers. But

Valverde made a bid: 'Be baptized only, and you shall not be burnt; you shall be strangled instead.' The Inca gave way. Face to face with the frightful agony of death by burning, his spirit quailed. The minister of Christ was granted permission to sprinkle him with water. It was August 13, 1532, the Feast of St. John the Baptist. In memory of the forerunner, the Monarch received the name of John. 'John, I baptize thee——' The garrote was affixed, and the Inca expired.

These scenes of treachery and bloodshed, masked with a show of legality and religious principle, make the Spanish Empire one of the most nauseating studies of history. If we would know, by observation, what Spanish colonial government is like when the principles that dominate it are allowed full development, we are so fortunate as to have a model to our hand—one that grew out of the adventures of Magelhan.

Magelhan was a Portuguese, for whom his native country could find no adequate employment. He offered his services to Spain, and was entrusted with the pilotage and command of a naval expedition to the coast of South America, in the course of which he discovered the Straits that have borne his name ever since.

The record of this expedition can hardly be cited under the history of the Portuguese Empire, for the ships were Spanish and the money that paid its expenses was Spanish. It is hardly fair to give the credit of it to Spain; for, as usual, the hard work, the unremunerative and risky work of exploration, the anxiety and responsibility, were all borne by a Portuguese. Still, the expedition must be noted, for it had very important results— the opening up of the South Seas. As it was Spain that profited exclusively by the discovery, it seems, on the whole, more proper to record the incident in this chapter.

Magelhan, then, passed the Horn, and discovered the islands of the South Seas. He perished in a skirmish with the natives of one of the islands; but the profit of his work remained to Spain; and even to this day that country enjoys the possession of a group of wealthy and populous islands whose discovery is owing to Magelhan, and where we may observe, untrammelled by the criticisms of the press, undisturbed (except for once by England) by foreign conquest, unshaken by whispers of heresy, the true Spanish notions of government in full action. The kind of government that Spain thinks it desirable to set up and preserve is the Government of Manila.

Besides Manila and her other possessions in the South Seas, Spain had claims in another direction—claims which were often urged with some show of seriousness, but which could not prevail against the more assertive ambitions of France and England.

At the death of the Inca there was present an officer—a companion of Pizarro's—one De Soto. In later life De Soto discovered the Mississippi. It would not be correct to say that he explored any great part of what are now the Southern States of North America. But his wanderings extended over a large surface, and it was in consequence of them that Spain always claimed the northern shore of the Gulf of Mexico as Spanish ground. De Soto died there, and his journeys had really no pretensions to be a conquest; but this expedition has to be noticed, because it led later on to diplomatic friction between Spain and Powers that did something more than wander through the valley of the Mississippi.

With these exceptions, and also with the partial exception of Paraguay, Spanish history is all like the story of Mexico and Peru—a monotonous record of plunder and slaughter. It is as uninteresting as Turkish history. It is even more uninteresting, for the Turks and their fellow Musulmans often built cities which were miracles of beauty, and devised systems of legislation and social life which were a great improvement on what they supplanted. But the Spaniard's one notion was destruction: what was Castilian in the world was good, the rest was naught. No Turk was ever more stupid or more brutal. The Spanish Empire long held the attention and the admiration of the world, on account of the large sums of money poured into

Europe in consequence of its foundation, and of the immense tracts of country that came to be marked as Spanish on the map of the world. At its greatest extent it included, besides very extensive dominions in Europe, the whole of South and Central America with the exception of Brazil, the West Indian Islands, some parts of what is now the United States of America, and some islands of the South Seas. But it is not by reason of its wide extent that we must deem an empire great. Were it so, China would be the greatest of empires. It is surely by reason of the greatness of soul, or loftiness of life displayed by its founders and enjoined on its subjects. Not one single ennobling or inspiring idea went to the making of the Spanish Empire.

Greed and lust—lust of blood and greed of gold—were the names in which the Spaniards wrought all their deeds, although they shouted very different ones the while. It is worthy of remark that all the enterprise, the difficult, dangerous, and (most significant of all) unremunerative work of discovery or adventure was not done by Spaniards. It was only when there appeared to be a chance of making money quickly that a Spaniard would move at all. Even then he moved slowly and suspiciously. The words 'chivalrous zeal,' 'missionary enterprise,' 'crusading ardour' can no more be applied to Cortez and Pizarro than to Timúr or Bajazet. The Spaniards fell on the New World like a devastating horde, and dashed it out of existence. When we recall what the New World was, we realize that the crimes of Spain are unpardonable. When we recall the intense and peculiarly vivid life that pulsed through the realms of Montezuma and Atahuallpa, the innumerable lessons that we of Europe could have gleaned from observation of their laws, their life, their customs, their history, and their arts, and when we remember that Spain has destroyed for ever any chance that we can profit by them, it is impossible to read with patience the panegyric that every historian has lavished on the Empire of Spain.

It is always maintained that the Spaniards

should be pardoned much because they effectually converted the New World from Paganism to Christianity. It is true that they did so: they converted America to Christianity in precisely the same way as the early Caliphs converted Africa from Christianity to Islam—by terror of death. When we recall the conversion of America we must indeed keep a sorrowful silence over the destruction of the African churches, for in the person of the Spaniard Christianity showed itself as low as Islam—lower even, for when the convert had once said ' There is no God but God, and Muhammad is the prophet of God,' he was treasured as a man by his conquerors. But Spain never rested satisfied until she had stamped out of her new subjects every vestige of the qualities that go to make men and women. Not until she had terrified the thriving intelligent pagans of Mexico and Peru into a herd of trembling slaves who attended Mass, was she satisfied.

Nothing is more astonishing in history than that the two nations—the Spanish and

Portuguese—should have lived so long together, and such near neighbours, should both have founded empires, and should have remained in such strong contrast to one another: the Portuguese eager to take any trouble for the sake of extending his knowledge of the world, content with moderate gains, eager to fraternize with new nations, thinking always of how best to gain their sympathy and regard; the Spaniard dull and savage, moved only by the greed of gold or, like vultures, by the reek of death; stamping out with maniac ferocity everything that was not Castilian, enslaving, slaughtering, destroying; and all with a heavy and joyless greed and spite. The history of the expansion of Portugal, however badly told, can never be anything but exciting and romantic. The loftiest talents have been employed on the other hand in writing the history of the expansion of Spain, have eagerly taken up the brief of Spain, and have been so wrapped up in their brief as to state without any apparent consciousness of absurdity that what the

Spaniards did in America was not as bad as what the English did in Spain. All is of no avail. It is only with frequent intervals of nausea that we can plod through the dreary story; we wade through blood and crime, and in the end we arrive at nothing but the temporary enrichment of Philip II.'s treasury. It is for this that Mexico and Peru were blotted out.

To the eternal disgrace of Christianity we must recall what the Cuban chief said when exhorted to change his faith : 'I thank my gods that I am going, as you say, to hell, for there I shall, at any rate, meet no Christians!'

IV.
THE LOST EMPIRE OF FRANCE.

IV.

THE LOST EMPIRE OF FRANCE.

'La colonization est pour la France une question de vie ou de mort; ou la France deviendra une grande puissance africaine, ou elle ne sera dans un siècle ou deux qu'une puissance européenne secondaire; elle comptera dans le monde, à peu près comme la Grèce ou la Roumanie comptent en Europe.'

So says M. Leroy-Beaulieu; and M. Leroy-Beaulieu's judgments, especially a severe judgment like the above, must be most attentively weighed by anyone who would form an opinion as to whether France has an Imperial future or not.

We may be permitted to doubt whether,

from some points of view, France can ever become a second-rate Power. The world owes her, and must continue for many centuries to come to owe her, too much for that to be possible. But if France is to base her claim to the rank of a first-rate Power on the founding of a world State after the model of the British Empire, nothing is more certain (if the past and the present are any guides to the future) than that this claim will grow harder and harder to establish with every year that passes away. We have seen that the driving force of the Portuguese Empire was thought. The driving forces of the Spanish Empire were more simple, being the primitive but tremendous impulses of lust and greed.

The driving force of the French Empire was adventure. For several centuries France had continued to throw off a series of brilliant men who were carried to the ends of the earth by the love of inquiry or the love of sport. These men were gifted, hardly with an exception, with grandiose and noble ideas, and with admirable powers of exposition by which to make their aims known to their countrymen.

They were often good soldiers and able diplomatists; individually they got on well with native tribes. In a word, they were ideal pioneers of a Colonial Empire, and a sort of empire they did succeed in establishing. But, seeing they were in the field before us—in some cases a hundred years before us—and that they came of a country much more populous than the British Isles, the empire that they founded ought to have been impregnably strong by the time that England came to attack it. That it was not impregnably strong was due to the fact that the great colonial pioneers of France did not receive adequate support from the old country.

The people of Portugal were drawn into the path of colonial enterprise by the sublime genius of Henry the Thinker, and were guided to great deeds by the sagacity of successive Portuguese kings. The people of Spain entered on their career of devastating conquest drawn on by the dazzling dreams of a great fortune quickly acquired. Their monarchs were indifferent to their enterprise, but did not throw any obstacle in its way so long as their own interests were secured. Both empires were national enterprises, but the Portuguese succeeded through the efforts of their kings, and the Spaniards in spite of their kings.

The Kings of France had very little to do with founding or developing the colonial empire of France, but this was not necessarily a fatal weakness, as we have seen in the case of Spain. A national movement cannot be arrested by the indifference of a monarch. The fatal weakness of the empire of France was this : That it never was a national movement. The French pioneers of empire showed the way, but no great rush of men followed in their footsteps. Their deeds, when they became known in France, aroused no general enthusiasm. At most, they attracted the fleeting attention of a Minister, or became objects of commercial interest to a clique of speculators in the capital. Hence the story of 'The Lost

Empire of France' is for the most part the history of the unsupported efforts of a few great men.

The greatest of all these was Samuel Champlain, the founder of Quebec. Champlain received a military education, and did well in the service; but his talents were rather solid than brilliant, and at the age of thirty-two he had filled no higher post than the respectable but not very important one of Quartermaster. In this capacity, however, he had earned the esteem of two marshals, D'Aumont and De Brissac, and had so impressed the thrifty Henry IV. that he had earned a pension ' to attach him to the royal household.' Being for the moment out of employment, and removed from the necessity of earning a living, he made a journey to the New World. This was with the object of acquiring information that might be of use to his Sovereign. He made his way to Cadiz, and sailed thence, in the year 1599, to Hispaniola. He kept a diary, and noted in extraordinary detail, and with singular accuracy of observation, everything that he saw. He was an excellent draughtsman; he catalogued the natural features of the islands and the mainland. He rarely made comments on what he saw, but when he did they were pregnant comments indeed.

At Portobello, 'the most evil and pitiful residence in the world,' he pointed out that the obvious thing for the Spaniards to do was to cut a waterway across to Panama, seventeen leagues off, and save 1,500 leagues of sea. So Champlain anticipated M. de Lesseps by two centuries and a half. The furthest point that he reached was the city of Mexico, which then contained a population of about 100,000, including 15,000 Spaniards, or about one-third of its population in Aztec days, sixty years before. 'All these Indians,' he writes, 'are of a very melancholy humour'—no wonder—'but have nevertheless very quick intelligence, and understand in a short time whatever may be shown to them, and do not become irritable whatever action or abuse may be done or said to them.' Before the day of Cortez the Aztecs were very easily irritated, but when Champlain saw them they had been well dragooned; they had learnt the dire consequences of being irritated with a Spaniard.

He returned to France after an absence of three years, and found that his old friend, the Governor of Dieppe, was planning an expedition to explore and settle Canada. If Champlain had been valued before, he was now doubly valued, and was immediately selected to be one of the leaders of the expedition. From this year, 1603, to his death at Quebec in 1635 he was continually backwards and forwards between Canada and France, with the exception of a stay of five weeks in London after the fall of Quebec, at the end of the year 1629. Thirty-two years of the labour of such a man as Champlain, commencing at the time when he was in the pride of his strength and already of ripe experience, ought to have settled the new colony on an impregnably solid basis. As a matter of fact, it left Quebec a rudely-fortified stockade, affording a scanty shelter to, at most, 200 men, who subsisted on supplies sent out from France.

In January, 1627, he notes the death of a settler named Hebert, the first man who lived by what he cultivated, and in 1627 Quebec had been founded for nineteen years. It was not Champlain's fault that the colonists did not grow their own wheat; to induce them to do so was one of the prime objects of his policy, but his masters in France would not allow it.

He had many masters. First there was the King, to whose favour he owed his position; then came the Viceroy, whose deputy he was—and it is a most remarkable tribute to Champlain's equanimity that he was the trusted deputy of seven successive viceroys—the Comte de Soissons, the Prince de Condé, the Marquis de Thémines, the Prince de Condé again, the Duc de Montmorency, the Duc de Ventadour, and the Cardinal Duc de Richelieu.

The King did very little, one way or the other, but the viceroys drew large profits from their post, which was worth from

70,000 to 100,000 livres. They were always highly-placed men, and, after the bad habit of these and later days, they resided in France, and concerned themselves with nothing but the profits of their charge. Towards the expenses of the colony they contributed nothing. The merchant adventurers were a third set of masters. They found the money for the ships and stores, and were an exceedingly jealous, exacting, litigious body of shopkeepers. They came from Rouen and St. Malo, and at first endeavoured to associate with the men of La Rochelle. But the Rochellais quarrelled over the terms of the articles of association, and, having commenced proceedings in the Courts of Law at Paris, took the additional precaution of organizing a piratical expedition on their own account. 'Very bad subjects,' Champlain calls them, as well he might, even if he had not been an ardent Churchman, and the Rochellais equally ardent Protestants.

Between viceroys, paymasters, and pirates, to say nothing of Indian wars and the inherent difficulties of the Canadian climate, one might well wonder that anything moved at all. It needed no less a man than Champlain to save the movement from being stifled in its birth. A portrait of him that still exists shows him to have been in personal appearance something like our Strafford, but with a humorous cast of features that perhaps helps to explain his success. His first voyage was undertaken in the year 1603. It was not exactly a voyage of discovery, for the coast of North America had been constantly visited by Frenchmen for a century past.

And yet, although the French were quite as daring explorers as the Portuguese, they had nothing like the results to show for their labours that the Portuguese had in half the time. The countries that they visited were far more full of promise than the unhealthy West African coast; but in France there was no Prince Henry. With proper guidance and support the French would have colonized from Florida to the St. Lawrence by Champlain's time. We can count eighteen separate expeditions between the years 1504 and 1603.

each of them manned by stout-hearted sailors
and guided by capable captains, including no
less a man than Jacques Cartier, who got as
far as the present site of Montreal as early
as the year 1534.

In those early days the Indians were not
unfriendly, and nothing but a guiding hand
in the old country was needed to have
developed the nucleus of a great French
State on the Atlantic shore of North
America. One great difficulty, however,
we must not overlook. In Prince Henry's
days the Church was not yet torn by
schism; in Champlain's time the strife between Catholic and Protestant was at its
height. It was owing to this miserable
state of things that one determined attempt
to colonize Florida came to nothing.

As early as 1565 no fewer than 600
French Protestants sailed in a fleet fitted
out by private enterprise, and settled in
Florida. They might have chosen a more
fortunate climate for their great experiment;
but, still, 600 men and women formed a large
body of colonists, and allowed of a good deal

of wasting. No doubt they would have received recruits with time, and so would have been able to endure, without breaking down, the first hard lessons of settlers in a new land.

The Spaniards fell on them from the secure vantage-ground of 'the Islands,' and massacred them all with horrid barbarity. Those who did not perish in the Spanish onslaught were hanged; and this legend was affixed to their gallows: 'These men are not hanged as Frenchmen, but as heretics.' This was a delicate way of intimating that no diplomatic offence was intended. Two or three men managed to escape the slaughter, and made their way to Europe, where they cried out for vengeance; but Spanish dexterity had forestalled them at Court, and although diplomatic representations were made, it was evident that no reparation would be offered by the Court of Madrid. Silently and swiftly the Protestants took their revenge. A second expedition was privately equipped. No gewgaws for Indian chiefs, or spades for cultivation, did they take in their cargo, but muskets and ammunition in plenty; scaling ladders, swords and daggers. They fell on the Spanish settlers in Florida even as the Spaniards had fallen on their brethren of the Reformed Faith. They stormed the stockade that stood on the site of their once promising colony, and hanged all their prisoners with this grim legend round their necks: 'These men are not hanged as Spaniards, but as traitors, robbers, and murderers.'

The memory of these dark scenes was strong in Champlain when, in the first year of the reign of James I., he sailed across the Atlantic and landed at Tadoussac. He seems to have taken the squabblings in the old country as part of the day's work. He did not murmur that the magnificent young gentlemen whose deputy he was (the Prince de Condé was Viceroy at twenty-four, the Duc de Montmorency at twenty-five) should look for, and in fact take, very large sums from an enterprise to which they contributed nothing. He recognized that the protection of their great name gave stability to his work, and shielded him from his paymasters — the merchants of Rouen, who found the money and expected such terribly large profits from his labours.

But what Champlain was determined to put an end to was the scandalous and disastrous bickering between Catholic and Protestant. He himself was an ardent Churchman, and spent a great deal of his time in instructing natives in the dogmas of the Christian faith. It was unspeakably mortifying and shocking to him to see the priest and the pastor come to blows over their arguments, while the Indians cheered and took sides as at a prize-fight. He accordingly forbade the Protestants who sailed with him to sing psalms or to engage in common prayer. The French Protestants were most devoted to their reformed faith, and threatened a mutiny. If Champlain had been a Spaniard he would have faced the mutiny; in which case the cause of the French colonization in Canada would probably have gone down in a bloodstained derelict in the Atlantic. But Champlain's whole soul was devoted to the colonial expansion of France, and though a good Catholic, he compromised rather than lose a man. It was a most remarkable testimony to the conciliatory nature of the man that any compromise should have been possible, considering the times and the subject. Singing psalms he would not endure, and his men would not submit to be deprived of their common prayer. So common prayer was tolerated, and psalm-singing suppressed. 'Of a bad debt collect what you can,' he wrote home.

His colonists, of all faiths, were a worthless lot. Their diversions were drinking and squabbling with the Indians. They wastefully lived on the stores exported from France, often reducing themselves to the verge of starvation. Their lawless conduct was loudly exclaimed against by the Basques and Rochellais, whose complaints were all the louder because they were themselves outside the Canadian 'ring.' It was to quiet these outcries that, at the end of the year 1607, De Monts' commission was cancelled. De Mont was a most patriotic gentleman, who had subscribed 100,000 livres out of his private fortune towards the expenses of the Canadian expeditions, and had himself sailed in them. He was granted a contingent compensation of 6,000 livres. Nothing daunted, although highly indignant, he fitted out another ship, and Champlain again sailed for Canada, this time resolutely determined to work up the St. Lawrence to China.

This plan had been strictly enjoined by Francis I. on Jacques Cartier, who got no further on the road than Montreal. But Champlain was in possession of positive information. The English explorers, so he was informed, had actually discovered the North-West Passage; although, owing to the fact that they had been wrecked and subsequently massacred by Indians, their secret had died with them, except that it was in the hands of Champlain's informant. On May 27, 1613, he started from Montreal with four Frenchmen and an Indian guide, one of the Frenchmen being Nicholas Vignau; he it was who had undertaken to pilot Champlain to China. When the party had penetrated seventy-five leagues of country, and suffered endless hardships, Vignau fell at Champlain's feet, and confessed that he had invented the yarn from beginning to end.

Prior to this ridiculous and vexatious fiasco, Champlain had married. It is the most inexplicable act of his life. The marriage contract exists, and shows that there was no money on either side. The young lady was Hélène Boullé, after whom the Isle St. Hélène in the St. Lawrence was named. She was of no great family—her father was Secrétaire de la Chambre du Roi —and to crown all, Champlain was forty-three and his bride was twelve. Madame Champlain stayed with her parents while her husband was occupied in Canada, and did not join him there until ten years after her marriage.

Champlain's scheme of colonization was to form a strong nucleus of French settlers, and to group around them bodies of friendly Indians. It was probably unavoidable that he should take some side in the native wars, and he invariably sided with the Algonquins against the Iroquois. But with his gentle temper, and his genuine desire to sympathize with the Indians, he would have quickly made friends with other tribes than the Algonquins, if his masters would have allowed him to do so. There was nothing to be expected from the merchant adventurers, for they openly declared that they could have no part in any scheme that tended to the 'independence,' as they called it, of the settlements; they did not want the colonists to be capable men : all that they wished was that they should be docile agents for the fur trade.

Better things might have been expected from the viceroys, but the great post of Viceroy of Canada was unfortunately swept one way or the other by all the cross-currents of Paris political life. On one occasion Champlain landed at Havre, eagerly looking forward to obtaining the help of the Prince de Condé in developing Montreal. He found the Viceroy in prison, whither he had been conveyed by the Marquis de Thémines, who had been ordered to arrest him, and was made a Marshal as his reward on the same day. The Marquis de Thémines was a man who had long passed the age when men take a romantic interest in the affairs of this life.* From the spoils of Monsieur le Prince, the Marshal arrogated to himself the office of Viceroy of Canada ; not because he took any interest in Canada, but because he was sure that the Prince de Condé had not made enough out of his post, and that he would be able to make a great deal more himself. Accordingly he proposed to raise the price of furs, and to augment the gratifications payable to the Viceroy and his deputy,. especially those payable to the Viceroy.

The merchant adventurers were furious, and a violent quarrel ensued between the trading companies and the Viceroy. Champlain would have nothing to say to either

* He was sixty-three when he arrested the Prince de Condé, and had already been a Knight of the Holy Ghost for nineteen years.

side. He had come to France to raise money for Montreal, and as it was soon made manifest to him on all sides that no money would be forthcoming, he quietly returned to Canada, and left his paymasters to fight over the profits that he was about to earn for them.

He made his voyage, and returned home to find Thémines and the merchants still, after a lapse of twelve months, squabbling over the price of fur. This time he gravely remonstrated with both, and the merchants appear to have been so far made ashamed of themselves that on the remonstrances of their servant they allowed him to choose a picked band of eighty colonists. When taking them back to Canada Champlain was for the first time accompanied by his wife, and the settlement looked as if it might have some expansive power within it.

But this was a delusion. After a year in Canada, Champlain came back, and found that Montmorency, who was now Viceroy, had resigned his post in favour of the Duc de Ventadour. The incessant changes of

Viceroy were most damaging to the cause of colonization, and in this case particularly so.

The Duc de Ventadour was a very pious man, most anxious for the propagation of the Faith, and it appears that he was himself actually in Holy Orders. He was the Jesuits' man, the Duc de Montmorency not being sufficiently zealous in their cause. No man could have been more genuinely and deeply anxious to see the Faith flourish than Champlain. It was owing to his exertions that the Jesuits had obtained their first footing in Canada in 1615. He approved of their energy, he admired their character, and he earnestly furthered their designs wherever he could do so. But it was really too much that they should nominate the Viceroy. Champlain was duly confirmed by the Duke as Deputy-Viceroy, but he could get no help for his struggling colony, and it is a most painful example of the extent to which the greed and folly of the home authorities had lamed his enterprise, that on returning to Canada as Ventadour's deputy, he found only twenty-four men fit for work in his entire colony.

Then came the crash that he had long been anticipating. A little knot of adventurers in London fitted out an expedition, and set out to conquer Canada. They were commanded by David Kirk, a daring man, but Champlain showed so bold a face in his adversity that he actually frightened Kirk into giving up his project of conquering Quebec. He contented himself with destroying the fleet, laden with provisions, that he encountered in the St. Lawrence. This was a less heroic feat than a siege or a battle, but it was quite as effective as a victory, for it reduced Champlain and his little band almost to the verge of starvation. Kirk was really ignorant of the amount of damage that he had done, and had no idea that Quebec was actually at his mercy. A Frenchman gave him this valuable information.

The first English expedition against Canada took place in 1628. A year previously Richelieu had taken the affairs of the colony in hand. He swept away the companies, bought out the Duc de Ventadour, shut the Jesuits out of all influence in the affairs of Canada, and declared himself, and made himself, supreme director of colonial affairs, with the title of Grand Master and Superintendent of Navigation and Commerce.

Enraged at the loss of profits that he and his like had so long enjoyed, a disappointed speculator betrayed to David Kirk the true condition of the colony. In 1629 a second English expedition appeared in the St. Lawrence before Richelieu had time to arm or provision the place. There was no help for it; Champlain must surrender. On August 21, 1629, the English flag was hoisted over Quebec. Champlain was most courteously entreated and shipped to England. He made Plymouth on November 20, and the port of London nine days later. He at once sought out M. de Châteauneuf, the French Ambassador, and cast about for some flaw in the treaty of surrender. He soon found one. It appeared that the attack had been made at a time when France and England were, in fact, at peace. This was enough for Champlain. His stay in London lasted only five weeks. He hurried to Rye, crossed to France, and laid his case before the Duc de Richelieu.

On the one side was English enterprise—that best of all enterprise, private energy—possession, which in such matters more than in all others is nine points of the law, and Charles I. On the other side was a technical diplomatic advantage, with Champlain and Richelieu to urge it. It is hardly necessary to say that Richelieu had his way. Kirk was consoled with a knighthood, and by the Treaty of St. Germain-en-Laye, signed on March 29, 1630, Canada was restored to France.

Three years later Champlain sailed from Dieppe for the last time, and on Christmas Day, 1635, he died.

Great and angry emphasis has been laid upon Champlain's religion by advocates belonging to two opposite parties. It is only right to state that there is authority for drawing precisely the opposite conclusion as to Champlain's religion to that set forward in the preceding pages. Champlain is as often described as a Protestant as a Catholic. The passages proving him to have been a Catholic are alleged to have been inserted by interested narrators. It is a point worth disputing, for Samuel Champlain was a man whose character any religion might be proud to have formed. But from the point of view of this history it is perfectly immaterial. Whether priests or pastors trained the youthful Champlain, they trained a boy who became one of the greatest and best of the sons of France. Among her colonial statesmen he must stand in the first rank, if not in the first place.

A very different man was La Salle, the second discoverer of the Mississippi. If Champlain's talents were solid La Salle's were brilliant. It was La Salle who first imagined the vast design that afterwards so alarmed the elder Pitt—the design of connecting the Canadian Lakes with the Gulf of Mexico by a chain of forts along the valley of the Mississippi, and so rounding off the whole of the Eastern portion of the continent into a mighty French State. The effect of this plan, if carried out, would be to crowd the rising English settlements on the Atlantic sea-board into the space between the Alleghanies and the ocean. There was also a very good chance that the English might ultimately be edged off the continent altogether.

This is the kind of scheme that has always attracted Frenchmen. It appeals at once to their intelligence and their imagination. It gives them a grand objective that may be pursued steadily for generations, if not centuries, and all the time it holds before their eyes boundless possibilities of wealth and power. It is an ideal that they are pursuing in Africa at the present moment. It will always attract a people at once intelligent and imaginative. But it is an ideal that is apt to lead its pursuers to overlook the simple facts before them. In La Salle's case it was a wonderful flight of imagination, for the Mississippi was not even explored at the time when he proposed to use its waters as a link to connect Canada with Mexico.

Louis XIV., who deserves the title of Great much more than we are accustomed to admit, had laid down rules for the development of his colony of Canada, which were based on the facts of the case, and not from flights of imagination. He had instructed his officers that, considering the rigours of the climate and the dangers from Indians, it was highly inadvisable to allow indiscriminate colonizing. No village must be far from its next neighbour, the strength of the settlers must be concentrated, and no isolated posts permitted.

La Salle's plans were, of course, in exact opposition to the King's. If any restrictions upon colonizing are desirable, Louis' regulations were the wisest that could possibly have been devised. The entire population of Canada would not, at that time, have sufficed to plant settlements along the banks of the Mississippi in the way that La Salle desired to see. But there was no harm in exploring the river and in making sure that it did actually communicate with the Gulf of Mexico. This La Salle achieved, and on April 9, 1682, planted the flag of France at the mouth of the Mississippi and founded the State of Louisiana, christening it after his master, the King.

He returned to France, and was well, but not enthusiastically, received. Louis was at the height of his glory, having pursued for twenty years, unchecked, the career of European conquest to follow which he had early turned aside from Colbert's plans for colonial expansion. La Salle was to the world of Paris in the year 1682 very much what a second or third rate African explorer would be in the world of London 200 years later.

However, his second expedition was equipped, and he set sail for America, this time with the intention of sailing up the Mississippi from the Gulf of Mexico, and so confirming his previous knowledge of the river's course. It was on this expedition that the vices of La Salle's character showed themselves so unfortunately. Able and daring he undoubtedly was, but he was intensely vain and imperious, and had no power of awakening the sympathy or enthusiasm of his subordinates.

In the little-known waters of the Mexican Gulf his ship went astray; his pilots missed the mouth of the Mississippi, and landed him some hundreds of miles to the westward. An overland journey of extreme anxiety and hardship was commenced, and La Salle was not equal to the task of leading it. He was assassinated by his enraged and disappointed followers on March 20, 1687. His grand achievement was the foundation of the colony of Louisiana. During his lifetime he must have felt that he had been hardly treated by his King, and had accomplished nothing. Nevertheless, his work long remained, and of such as La Salle is the colonial empire of France.

This, then, was the scheme of the colonial empire of France in the Americas: Firstly, Canada, by which was meant a little knot of settlements on the lakes; secondly, the long valleys of the Ohio and the Mississippi, ending with Louisiana, which was held in force, in order to seal the mouth of the river from attacks by Spain. Canada was to expand northwards to the Pole, and south-eastwards to the Atlantic. The line of the Mississippi was to thrust eastwards to the Atlantic. The adventures of France in the West Indian Islands form a separate episode, which may be left for the present. The history of the mainland is the principal part of the story.

We are accustomed to consider the continent of North America as divided into two parts—Canada and the United States. The situation in early days was much less simple. South-east of French Canada lay New Amsterdam, a Dutch settlement, side by side with English settlements. The Dutch were quiet neighbours, extremely tenacious of their own rights, but not expansive or encroaching. Not so the English in Hudson's Bay. Not only were they more daring than the Dutch, but the country that they controlled was a fur-country, which was much more highly valued by French Canadians than the agricultural settlements on the Atlantic coast. Hudson's Bay, therefore, was early marked out for acquisition by the French.

But it was one thing to mark out Hudson's Bay for absorption into Canada, and quite another thing to absorb that immense and valuable territory. Of the prior rights of the English there could not be any doubt. The bay was discovered by Henry Hudson in the year 1610,* and was mistaken at the time for the North-West Passage to China. The discovery of this passage was the grand object of Hudson's life. By a most curious accident Hudson, travelling north on this quest, passed Champlain, travelling south on the same errand, in the year 1610; the great explorers were within fifty miles of each other. Although Hudson's Bay did not prove to be useful as a waterway to the East, it became the centre of a valuable and expanding fur-trade. The shores of the bay were dotted here and there with forts, and there was no talk of disputed rights

* This was a re-discovery, the first discovery having taken place in the year 1498.

there until the year 1682—the year of the foundation of French influence at the extreme south of the continent.

Hudson's Bay was finally confirmed to the English by the Treaty of Utrecht, but only after thirty-two years of determined struggle, the French attacking and the English defending. The diplomatic argument employed by the French was an extremely ingenious one. It went back to the Treaty of St. Germain-en-Laye, by which, as we have seen, the combined genius of Champlain and Richelieu rescued Canada from the grip of the English expedition of David Kirk. It will be remembered that this treaty was the beginning of a new era for French Canada, an era inaugurated by the foundation of Richelieu's Company of One Hundred.

This company was granted exclusive trading privileges up to the Arctic circle, and it was argued that, as Hudson's Bay lay between Canada and the Arctic circle, it was plain that, as the Treaty of St. Germain-en-Laye recognized the Company of One

Hundred, the French rights to Hudson's Bay were established as long ago as 1633.

It was a very good point, and if colonial matters had been decided in those days by taking good points, very likely French Canada would have run up to Hudson's Bay, and the colony would have got rid of one dangerous neighbour. Even as it was, the rights of the Hudson's Bay traders were seriously prejudiced—notably, at the Treaty of Ryswick. But it was not only or even chiefly diplomatic activity that was stirred up by the rivalry of France and England in North America. When the seventeenth century was three-quarters past, the French became very active in Canada ; we shall see why presently. In the direction of Hudson's Bay they made one highly-successful effort to oust us.

In the year 1686 D'Iberville expelled us altogether from Hudson's Bay. D'Iberville's expedition, like so many of those early colonial expeditions, was undertaken at a time when the home governments were actually at peace. James II. was King, and he had too many irons in the fire to take a very decided line in colonial policy. The question of Hudson's Bay was referred to a joint commission of French and English—Barillon and Bonrepaux representing France, Godolphin, Sunderland, and Middleton representing England—and the question was decided in favour of France. Thus, at the very moment when the murder of La Salle seemed to put an end for the time to all hopes of developing Louisiana, the French gained by a daring expedition, boldly supported in London, a far greater compensation in the extreme North.

War breaking out almost immediately, the French did not derive much profit from their new conquest, which was finally handed back to England in the year 1714. Thus ended, in complete failure, the plan of extending French Canada to the Arctic circle. A heavy burden was thrown on the little colony on the St. Lawrence—a burden which a colony of much greater expansive force would have been unable to support. But the French conceived themselves to be obliged to enter on these exhausting enterprises by an event that took place in the year 1677. This was the expedition of Robert Holmes, an expedition undertaken, like D'Iberville's, at a time of profound peace.

Holmes reduced the Dutch settlements on the West Coast of Africa, and then, crossing the Atlantic, attacked and captured New Amsterdam, which he re-named, in honour of the Duke of York, New York.

The West African settlements we were obliged to restore; they subsequently fell into the hands of the French, and Holland dropped out of the race for empire. But the same results did not take place in New York. The colony remained in our hands, and, although the French made several attempts to capture it, they did not succeed. The territory of New York ran up to Lake Ontario, the southern shore of which was claimed by the New York settlers, and the other English settlements pressed hard on the French possessions. It was clear that the grand struggle between France and

England in North America would have to be fought on the St. Lawrence. After the success of Holmes' expedition, the French were hemmed in between the English in the Atlantic States and the English in Hudson's Bay. They were probably right in turning on the weaker foe first. We have seen how they fared; but before we consider the result of their attempt to master the English settlements on their southern frontier, we may with advantage trace the history of their other great outpost, the colony of Louisiana.

La Salle's expeditions were, after all, little more than 'pointers.' When D'Iberville took up the work of his predecessor he was himself practically rediscovering the Mississippi. He was not sure that he had found it until he fell in with some Indians, who showed him a relic of La Salle's expedition —a prayer-book. D'Iberville was an active man, and covered a great deal of ground during his short stay in the colony. His two great fears were either an attack by Spain from the islands, or an attack by the

English from South Carolina. South Carolina was at that time the most southerly of the English colonies, but the English there made no move towards molesting the French in Louisiana. The Spaniards did send an armed force with hostile intentions to the mouth of the Mississippi, but, finding the French colony stronger than they expected, they contented themselves with a protest, alleging the prior claims of Spain, founded on De Soto's wanderings one hundred and fifty years before.

D'Iberville's great work was the foundation of Mobile. He died in the year 1706. In the year 1708 the total civilian population of Louisiana numbered 157, including women and children. As in Canada, so in Louisiana, the French were most reluctant to settle down to the labours of agriculture. Every immigrant expected to make a fortune, either by pearl fisheries or by discovering mines, and there were incessant squabbles among the colonial authorities, if that is not almost too large an expression.

In the year 1717 the colony seemed about

to take a new lease of life. The dominion was transferred to Law in perpetuity, with exemption from taxation for twenty-five years, and many trading privileges. From 800 to 1,000 immigrants landed, and in 1718 New Orleans was founded. Two years later came the collapse of Law's scheme, and a new period of depression for Louisiana. In 1732 the province became a royal domain, and in the same year a most menacing event took place, an event that, as we shall see, had most far-reaching effects, in that it roused the government on the St. Lawrence to new efforts—efforts that in their turn alarmed England, and brought about the expulsion of France from North America. Governor Oglethorpe founded the colony of Georgia.

So far as Oglethorpe was concerned, this was purely a benevolent undertaking; and as a benevolent undertaking it received generous support in London. But it also received Government support—for reasons not exclusively benevolent.

In the year 1732 South Carolina, the

most southerly of all the North American colonies, was still exposed to dangers arising from the jealousy of Spain.

Georgia, which was to lie south of South Carolina, would be an effective buffer against these attacks, and an annual grant of ten thousand pounds was voted in aid of Oglethorpe's project by Parliament in consideration of the obvious political advantage of strengthening our settlements on the Atlantic coast by the foundation of a new colony.

In so far, then, as Oglethorpe's action had any political meaning, it was directed against Spain and not against France. But France could not help weighing, very seriously, not only the present action of the English, but also what that present action portended in the future. It was now just fifty years since La Salle had discovered that the Mississippi emptied into the Gulf of Mexico, and since the scheme had been struck out of connecting the colonies on the St. Lawrence with Louisiana by the valley of the Ohio. During that fifty years the French had done almost nothing towards the realization of their ambition. A few stockades, strong enough to protect the defenders against a surprise by Indians, and called Mobile or New Orleans, and held by a few score soldiers and as many civilians, represented France in the valley of the Mississippi.

As for expansion eastwards to the Atlantic coast, there had been no attempt to do anything of the kind, for excellent reasons—there were not men enough. And now the French beheld themselves forestalled, and the English frontier extended to the latitude of Louisiana by means of a colony occupying the very ground that in their dreams the French had marked out for themselves. Moreover, the colony was not of the kind that the French were accustomed to found. It speedily showed an amount of 'spring' and self-reliance that was hardly surpassed by the French colonies on the St. Lawrence that had been in existence for a century. It actually attacked the Spaniards; and, though defeated in the attack, had strength enough to repel very gallantly the return assault.

A pushing, belligerent settlement of this kind was the last sort of neighbour that France desired in her southern colonies. The most disagreeable possibilities opened out; and it was determined to take seriously in hand the policy so long academically adopted as desirable, to shut the English off east of the Alleghanies, to line the Ohio and the Mississippi with forts, and to occupy those forts in force, and turn them into colonies by emigration from the older settlements as occasion served.

Activity on distant frontiers had not served the French well. In the extreme North the English, far from being expelled from Hudson's Bay, were more firmly established there than ever. In the extreme South the French not only had effected next to nothing with their colony of Louisiana, but saw themselves, as they supposed, menaced in their turn. There remained nothing but to try conclusions on the St. Lawrence; and here the chances were much more in favour of the French than they probably realized. For the English policy in Georgia and Hudson's Bay was controlled by the Home Government; whereas in the New England colonies the Home Government was at the mercy of the Provincial Assemblies.

The genius of the company of men who drafted the Constitutions of the United States half a century later has caused us to, in a measure, overlook the performances of the Provincial Assemblies at the time we are now considering. They showed no political capacity whatever. They were quarrelsome, exacting, and incapable. They not only showed no patriotism: they jeered at patriotism. Besides being incapable, they were disunited and mutually jealous. Accustomed as we are now to the vigorous statesmanship of our self-supporting colonies, to their forward policy, their magnificent self-reliance, their noble emulation in material progress, their pride in each other's achievements, their not infrequent chafing at the action of the Home Government, which they look on as leisurely and timid, it is with some difficulty that we realize that in the middle of the eighteenth century the situation was reversed. It was the Home Government that desired to push on, the Home Government that urged the danger of disunion, the Home Government that exhorted and implored the Provincial Assemblies to rise above a policy of sixpences, and take a view of politics that had, at any rate, some glimmer of statesmanship in it.

This state of things was the grand opportunity for the French. Their own colony was well in hand, and its policy firmly directed. Although greatly inferior in population to the English settlements, the latter were disunited, whereas Canada was one. Against the Home Government they could make no way—might they not succeed against the Provincial Government? The chance was a good one.

Their serious efforts commenced in the year 1747 with the appointment of Count de la Galissonière to be Governor of Canada. We must put out of our eyes the vast extent of the North American Continent, and endeavour to realize the comparatively small

area in which France and England fought
out their great struggle for the domination of
the whole. Heavy were the blows given and
taken by the two rivals before the battle on
the Heights of Abraham closed a struggle
that had lasted twelve years, from De la
Galissonière's appointment in 1747 to the fall
of Quebec in 1759.

Cape Breton, which (as the Duke of
Newcastle was so astonished to learn) was
an island, was French ground since the
Treaty of Aix-la-Chapelle. Nova Scotia was
English, and had been so since the Treaty
of Utrecht. Canada did not extend
practically beyond the extreme westerly
point of Lake Ontario, which was guarded
by Fort Niagara; the easterly end of the
lake was guarded by Fort Frontenac. The
colony of New York claimed the southern
shore of Lake Ontario, and had a fort,
strongly held, at Oswego, in the middle of
the southern shore. Montreal could be
approached up Lake Champlain, which was
closed at the north by Fort Ticonderoga; to
the south of Lake Champlain, on Lake

George, the English held Fort William Henry. Quebec was supposed to be unapproachable by the St. Lawrence, owing to the difficulties of navigation.

It was in this narrow arena that France and England thrust at each other during twelve years.

France may be said to have drawn first blood by the acquisition of Cape Breton, which gave her the commanding position of Louisburg—a very strong fortress. Six months later England founded the city of Halifax. This was one of the very few official colonizations by England. It was admirably effected and entirely successful. The close of the long war with France had thrown numbers of men and officers out of employment; and these men were emigrated to Nova Scotia and settled at Halifax. They numbered no less than 2,576 souls, and, being good material originally, they quickly took root and rapidly multiplied. It was a severe blow to France; for one of the chief points of the policy of De la Galissonière had been to re-acquire Nova Scotia, and so join

Cape Breton to Canada. The foundation of Halifax strengthened our grip on Nova Scotia ; so, turning aside from this part of the French plan of conquest, the new Governor, De la Jonquière, without loss of time, followed up the principal aim of his predecessor and turned to the Ohio.

Both De la Galissonière and De la Jonquière were distinguished sailors, and the former is famous in history for his capture of Minorca. In Canada he had laid down a forward policy for France in every direction. He took his policies in geographical order, beginning at the North with Hudson's Bay; here he did nothing. Halifax checked his plan of absorbing Nova Scotia; there remained two projects: to push down Lake Champlain into the heart of the English settlements, and to dominate the valley of the Ohio. Before giving over charge, he had formally proclaimed the sovereignty of the French King over the whole of these regions, and had openly announced his intention of securing the line of the Mississippi down to Louisiana.

Eight months after the foundation of Halifax, De la Jonquière took up this line of policy, and formally called on Governor Clinton of New York to forbid English subjects to trade on the Ohio. The Governor returned no reply; English traders persisted, and De la Jonquière consequently had them arrested and sent to Montreal. From this year the French went on from success to success. The arrest of peaceful English traders was nothing less than an outrage; but it was not likely to be resented by the kind of public opinion which was all that the English governors had to work on, and no move was made for three years. In the meantime, Fort Duquesne was founded, and the colonial borders were harried ever more and more by French Indians. The French got on very well with natives at that time; it is an art that they appear to have lost.

But they seem to have owed part at least of their influence to the license they allowed to the Indians. License to Indians in the hour of victory meant permission to burn, torture, and outrage their captives; the French allowed this.

The horrors of Indian warfare were an old-standing terror. They might have been suppressed as between French and English, but the French thought that harrying our borders was good policy. De Vaudreuil in particular insisted very strongly on its good effects. The question of humanity apart, it is probable that De Vaudreuil was wrong.

The new menace was the foundation of Fort Duquesne. This place, on the eightieth parallel of west longitude, at the junction of the rivers Alleghany and Monogahela, commanded both these rivers, and also the Ohio, which rises from their confluence. The Alleghany gave access to the French colonies, and the Monogahela, less readily, to the English colonies. The fort was named after the Marquis Duquesne, who had come out from France to be Governor of Canada in the year 1752, with definite instructions to drive the English out of the valley of the Ohio. It was completed in the year 1754; the net was fast closing round the English settlements. They made an attempt to break through—the attempt known to history as the disastrous expedition of General Braddock. A considerable armed force was directed on Fort Duquesne; it was defeated with great slaughter, and Braddock lost his life.

The French cause was clearly in the ascendant; it was time for England to strike a return blow. She struck it in Nova Scotia. This province had been English ever since the Treaty of Utrecht. It was largely populated by settlers of French extraction, who had been treated with the utmost indulgence. It is hardly credible, but is nevertheless the fact, that for forty-two years they had steadily refused to take the oath of allegiance to the English King. We overlooked their attitude, only inviting them from time to time to re-consider it. We even allowed them exemption from taxation, in the hope of winning them over by this moderate treatment. It was in vain; and it appears quite certain that their rebellious state of mind was largely fostered (grievous though it is to say) by their priests, every one of whom was a political emissary, and continually dangled before the eyes of his flock the hope of being one day reunited to Canada. In the meantime it was their religious duty to make things uneasy for England, and to hold out the right hand of fellowship to their brethren in Cape Breton, who were still French subjects. They succeeded so well in their exhortations that the English Government in the year 1755, driven to desperation by the very grave aspect of affairs in the American colonies, came to, and acted upon, a stern resolution : the plague spot must be cut out.

For the last time the oath of allegiance was tendered ; and on its being refused the entire French population, numbering some six thousand souls, was deported from Nova Scotia and scattered among the different New England colonies. Orders were issued to the different Governors to take steps ensuring that the expatriated families should not be permitted to reunite in any one place.

This was our return blow for Braddock's defeat. Nova Scotia, with the new settlement of Halifax thriving and prospering on the western coast, and with all the French malcontents expelled from the eastern coast, now became a solid wedge of English soil, driven in between the French in Canada, and the French in Cape Breton. The Home Government, by this vigorous action, had retrieved in the north-east something of what had been lost by Duquesne's action on the Ohio.

But France had at last realized that her grand opportunity was in the disunion of the New England States. Our action in Nova Scotia was, for the moment, a heavy blow; but if her own main action succeeded, and the English could be shut up between the Alleghanies and the sea, Nova Scotia would matter very little. Accordingly, she pursued her policy with ever-increasing vigour and success. In the summer of 1756 the Marquis de Montcalm, the new Governor of Canada, attacked and captured Oswego. Immense stores fell into his hands, with £18,000 sterling in silver, and over 1,600 prisoners. Oswego was razed to the ground; and Lake Ontario, with its two ends guarded by Forts Niagara and Frontenac, became a French lake. Montcalm spoke with contempt of the English resistance. The English in the New World, he said, were very different men from the same men in Europe. The colonies made no return blow, watching with sullen resignation the dominion of the continent passing from their hands.

The French pushed on, and in the next year, 1757, gained yet another victory. This time they followed up the third line of De la Galissonière's policy, and struck on Lake Champlain. Fort William Henry was captured, and the French allowed their Indian allies to commit frightful barbarities on the defeated garrison. The end of all things seemed at hand: Ontario was gone, the line of the Ohio was gone, and the French had pushed on into the very heart of the New England settlements. It seemed to be not so much a question whether the English should be shut up between the Alleghanies and the sea, as whether they would be permitted to remain in the continent at all, except as French subjects.

It was the brightest hour of the fortunes of France. It was not only that the acquisitions of France were brilliant and important : it was the complete demonstration of the impotence of the colonists to resist the French attack that was so full of promise for the French cause. Only a conjunction of four events could now wrest from France the exclusive dominion of North America : firstly, that the mother country should come to the help of the colonies ; secondly, that the help should be not only substantial, but overwhelming; thirdly, that the general in command should be, not some Court favourite, like Hill, not some incompetent senior, like Whitelocke, but a picked man, for the emergency was appalling ; fourthly, most important of all, that the English should have learnt the lesson that the French had learnt, and so skilfully turned to such important results—viz., that instead of tapping at outlying posts, we should strike at the heart of the French dominions, and at one blow conquer or be conquered.

All four conditions were fulfilled, for Pitt was the Minister, Wolfe the general, and Quebec the point of attack. On July 28, 1758, Louisburg fell. Between 5,000 and 6,000 French were taken prisoners; Cape Breton was ours, and the way up the St. Lawrence was open. But the lustre of this great achievement was dimmed by the news of yet another French victory. In attempting to throw back the French from their point of vantage on Lake Champlain, Abercrombie was heavily defeated at Ticonderoga with a loss of 2,000 men; George, third Viscount Howe, who is commemorated under the north-west tower of Westminster Abbey, was among the dead. Pitt was greatly depressed; for only a few weeks now remained in which to operate before the St. Lawrence was closed by the ice. Te Deums were chanted in the churches of Quebec in thankfulness for the victory and the approaching triumph of the cause of France. They were shortly to be succeeded by Misereres.

The victory of Ticonderoga was the last gleam of success that gilded the arms of France. Stung by the repulse, and determined to drown in action the fatal depression that had fallen on the spirits of the colonists, Bradstreet obtained leave to make yet one more attempt to threaten the French on the St. Lawrence. The expedition of Wolfe still delayed to attack, and we had sustained a bloody defeat on Lake Champlain; perhaps a move might be made on Lake Ontario.

On August 29 Fort Cataraqui (by Fort Frontenac) fell to the English. It was the first of a long series of successes. A fortnight later Quebec itself fell: Wolfe died, but Montcalm died also, and a blow was struck at the heart of the French settlements that left them prostrate. Early in the winter the dreaded Fort Duquesne was approached and found deserted. It was occupied by the English, and re-christened—in commemoration of the mighty genius who had inspired the whole campaign—Pittsburg.

In the next year Ticonderoga and Crown Point fell to Amherst, and Montreal to

Murray. Nothing remained to France but Louisiana—the *fons et origo mali*.

So ended the empire of France in North America. The French had a plan; the English had none. The French plan was perfectly feasible; it only failed because it was unsupported. Daring though the scheme may appear of connecting, in those early days, the settlements on the St. Lawrence with the Gulf of Mexico, there was nothing really insuperable in the obstacles to be overcome. Fort Duquesne, for example, could easily have been built fifty years before the date of its actual foundation, at a time when the English had not crept far from the coast. In the rather feeble and cross-grained temper of the Provincial Assemblies there would have been found no centre of opposition to this move; and the 'Protectorate'—to use the modern word—of the French being once recognized diplomatically, there could have been no opposition in Europe. 'Pegging out the claim' would have been even easier at the other end of the line; for the English were so far off that protests from them would have been ridiculous. France delayed, it is true; but when her scheme was once taken in hand seriously it had a rapid and startling success. The conjunction of the genius of Pitt and the genius of Wolfe was almost miraculous, and that conjunction alone it was that ruined the cause of France.

Louisiana—a *damnosa hereditas* indeed for France—had an eventful history, terminating in an episode that is worth studying. The colony was ceded to Spain in the year 1762, as the price of the Spanish alliance against England. It remained in the hands of Spain for forty years; and then became the centre of one of those intrigues that justly earned for Napoleon the nickname of Jupiter-Scapin. His dealings with Louisiana showed a truly Olympian vastness of design—a design that he worked out with the tortuous cunning of a rascally attorney. The problem was to raise money for the English war; and he began as far from his object as to offer the King of Spain a throne for a member of his family. The throne was to be formed out of the territories of Parma — territories that it is perhaps needless to say did not belong to France. So far, there was nothing in the transaction to awaken suspicion or to reveal Napoleon's object. It was natural that the King of Spain should desire to see another throne in his family; it was natural that Napoleon should feel flattered at the idea of creating a king, and keeping him waiting in his ante-chamber, as he actually did. The kingdom was formed—the kingdom of Etruria — and the Spanish Prince took possession.

Napoleon's price was the really very moderate price of the cession of Louisiana — a colony that had never profited any European Power yet. Spain made the cession without demur. Louisiana was indeed valueless to France as a colony. But Napoleon did not propose to re-open the question of French colonization in North America. Nor did he propose to offer the colony to any other European Power: he offered it to the United States, who would be, as he calculated, eager purchasers. He was right. They paid him three millions and a quarter sterling for an asset which he had acquired for nothing; so that the First Consul had the profit of paying this very large sum into his war-chest, and the pleasure of dealing England a shrewd thrust.

It is often made a matter of reproach to France that she has produced so many colonial adventurers. It has even been maintained that the scanty success enjoyed by France in her Imperial enterprises is largely to be ascribed to her superabundant crop of adventurers. It is chiefly French writers who take this view—writers who admire and envy the more solid results that have been attained by the comparatively plodding English. Such writers overlook the immense debt that England herself owes to her adventurers—her Raleighs, and Drakes, and Hudsons. France failed, not in consequence of her adventurers, but in spite of them. Adventurers not only are not harmful to a country seeking to found a colonial empire—they are indispensable to such a country; they are her pioneers. Without adventurers an empire cannot be founded, although it is true that in order to consolidate an empire so founded one of two subsequent conditions is indispensable—either a spontaneous outflow of settlers, or else a steady colonizing policy on the part of the Home Government.

France enjoyed neither of these advantages, and yet how nearly she succeeded! It is true that there was too much adventure altogether about the Canadian population: there were too many *coureurs de bois* among their scanty numbers. Nevertheless, the French colony founded by adventurers was more than a match for the English colony founded by settlers. But because France had begun too late to fill out this first sketch of a colonial empire, the slender fabric of the French colony went down before the dead weight of the English assault.

About the history of Canada we have to remark that there was a settled population sufficiently large, with permanent interests of sufficient magnitude, to neutralize one very painful feature of the French policy of adventure — the personal jealousy and rivalries of individuals. Of course there were such jealousies and rivalries, but they were neither so bitter in themselves nor so disastrous to France as the same painful incidents proved to be in India. On the whole, the policy of French Canada was free from these dissensions, and yet Canada passed over to England.

But France had her revenge. Not twenty years had passed after the fall of Quebec before she dealt a heavy return blow at England. She recognized the United States, and, by placing her navy in opposition to the navy of England, she finally severed the colonies from their mother-country. In North America, at the close of the long duel, France was a little more than quits.

On the mainland the contest for the dominion of the continent was almost exclusively between France and England. Holland dropped out of the running very early; Spain had comparatively trifling interests there. But in the vast and varied region of the West Indies all the colonizing races of the world struggled with each other for two centuries and a half. The shiftings of power in North America, although great, were definitely effected but seldom, and at rare intervals of time. But war in the West Indies never ceased, for when peace was officially concluded there still remained the buccaneers. The shiftings of power were not only frequent but kaleidoscopic, and if any attempt were to be made to record them nothing less than an encyclopædia would suffice. Nevertheless, we shall not lose much by passing them over, for they all depended in the past, as they must depend in the future, on the balance of sea-power. In the past, when the great fleet actions had been fought, the islands invariably fell, one by one, to the victors. So it will be in the future.

At the present day the West Indian Islands are held by Spain, France, Holland, and England. Spain, with the aid of 250,000 soldiers—or rather more than the whole army of India, native and English combined—still maintains a precarious dominion in Cuba. France holds Martinique and Guadaloupe, with some dependencies; Holland holds Curaçao, finally returned to her at the great peace; England holds the greater part of the remaining islands. The two great possessions of France, Martinique and Guadaloupe, have over and over again been English possessions, and have regularly been restored at the conclusion of peace. There is only one lesson to be learnt from all these incidents, and that is the very plain one that nothing is certain here except to the Power that commands the sea.

On the whole, there is little for France to regret in the West Indies. Any losses that she has sustained she has sustained as the direct consequence of the loss of sea-power, and without sea-power the most exalted genius for colonization would not have secured for her more than her present possessions.

Far different is the case with the East Indies, for French India is a great 'might have been,' which France must needs regret even unto this day. She has good reason to do so. British India is the greatest political achievement since the empire of Alexander. We are still too near to the colossal fabric to appreciate its grandeur. It is only down the perspective of centuries that the structure can be seen in its right proportions. Why is this not a French instead of a British Empire? The French were there before us; they possessed in a high degree the two qualities of intelligence and imagination, both of which are invaluable in such an enterprise; and these qualities had full play, without the neutralizing influence of a population of settlers—an influence which always tells in favour of England—for there was from the commencement no possibility of settling.

The reason may be found in the fatal weakness of a policy of pure adventure— a policy of which the characteristics, both good and bad, had untrammelled play in India, and the bad outweighed the good. As a rule, the English in India, although often personally inferior to their French rivals, pulled together. This was because they had a deeper sense of their duty towards each other than the French, and a stronger feeling of the obedience due to the home authorities. There resulted a sort of sense of discipline or service feeling, which, though rough, sufficed for the circumstances. All this was wanting to the French, and in consequence they simply cut each other's throats. We are accustomed to blame ourselves for the scurvy treatment that we dealt out to our great Indian pioneers, and to deplore their spirit of dissension among themselves. But we were a band of brothers compared to the French, whose personal vanity and inconceivable spite and envy towards each other were the real causes of their failure. Sea-power plays only a secondary part in this drama; there was at least one opportunity of founding a great French empire in India which sea-power could not have hindered, or even seriously annoyed when once it was founded.

It is only with partial reason that Macaulay complains of the treatment that India has received at the hands of English historians. No doubt Indian history has been dully treated, but if Macaulay is a brilliant exception, he only attained that position by laying on the colours, as he himself would have said, half an inch thick, by wild generalizations, by extravagant exaggeration, and by violent partisanship. The simple truth is that at this period Indian history is appallingly dreary.

When the great age of the Moguls was over, when Akbar had become a memory and Bijapur a ruin, Indian history subsides into a record of the scrambles of a horde of tenth-rate men. Some palace favourite, some soldier more daring than his fellows, seizes the Masnad, and rules precariously until a palace intrigue or the revolt of a provincial officer terminates his little day of glory by poison or steel, and his place is taken by a rascally rebel like himself—Zimri succeeds Omri. There is movement in plenty, but it is the movement of a seething cauldron—movement without advance.

In the broad wakes that the course of France and England traced in this *Male bolge* we find now one princelet, now another, swept to the surface, and for a time before he is once more submerged he remains visible and perhaps conspicuous. A great native ruler, a Haidar or a Shivají, arises but rarely, and his type is always the same—that of the ruthless soldier. India is no longer in labour with Akbars, and not as yet with Sálár Jungs. The old type of statesman no longer appears; the new type, trained under English influence, is not to be developed for another century and a half; the immediate future of the continent is clearly, from the commencement of the protracted period of collapse, in the hands of France or of England. There are three great epochs in each of which it appeared possible that France might wrest the Empire of India from England, or rather when it appeared almost certain that England would be expelled from the continent, where her foothold was not yet secure. In the first two of these decisive epochs, nothing but the mutual jealousy of Frenchmen ruined the cause of France; in the third, nothing but sheer good luck saved the cause of England.

These three epochs are:

1. The epoch of Dupleix and Labourdonnais.
2. The epoch of Lally, Bussy and D'Aché.
3. The epoch of Suffren.

These three epochs form three distinct crises in the fate of the East. They are to a certain extent linked together by the services of Bussy, who was conspicuous in the first two struggles between France and England, and who also gave some assistance to Suffren, although in 1782 he was only the shadow of the Bussy of thirty years before.

Just as in studying the lost Empire of France in North America we had to put out of our heads the vast extent of the American continent, and realize that the fate of the country was settled in a comparatively small area round the Canadian Lakes; so in regard to the lost Empire of France in India, we have to fix our attention on one small part of the Presidency of Madras. In this narrow space it was that France and England three times struggled for empire; here it was that France was three times thrown, and here it was that, even as late as Napoleon's Egyptian campaign, there were good hopes that the influence of France might be re-established through the sympathy of 'Citoyen Tippoo.' These hopes, which were well founded, were finally extinguished at the fall of Seringapatam, in the year 1799. This event took place one hundred years after the birth of Dupleix, who was actually a man of the seventeenth century. He was not a noble, as were most of the great French adventurers in the East: he was a man of good commercial connections; early initiated into the habits of trade, he remained throughout his life an excellent man of affairs.

But that was not all. Dupleix was a man of the highest capacity; and, conspicuous though he was as a man of business, he was still more remarkable as a political organizer, and a past grand master in the arts of Oriental intrigue. His general business training was supplemented by a long service, half commercial, half official, in the French places of business, Pondicherry and Chándanagar, and at the age of forty-three he found himself

Governor-General of the French Indies. The headquarters of the Government were at Pondicherry, about one hundred miles south of Madras. He immediately set to work to develop the trading centre of Pondicherry into something more dignified—into a great French State.

We are to remember that at this moment Clive and Warren Hastings were still both boys; Clive had just joined at Madras as a junior writer, and Hastings had just entered at Westminster; so long a start had this very great man of the two most illustrious empire makers of modern days. We are also to remember that in his dream of turning European traders into conquerors he was entirely original. We must also give Dupleix the credit for having discovered the means to realize his dream—the drilling of native troops on the European plan, and, by joining the forces so raised to small bodies of European troops, to form an army that would be irresistible by any native levies.

His success was immediate, complete, and startling. His weaknesses served him as well as his virtues, even better perhaps. He was excessively vain, but the circus-riding costume in which he indulged only passed for becoming pomp. Moreover, the people were too deeply impressed with Dupleix's personality to remark that he called himself, indifferently, by the Hindu title of Raja or the Mussulman title of Nawáb. He held gorgeous receptions which he was able to pay for without impairing the vast fortune that his shrewdness had enabled him to acquire. His spies were everywhere; in the inmost recesses of palaces the secrets of courts were whispered to the agents of Dupleix. The immediate influence that he exercised was already considerable; the indirect influence that he acquired by means of his genius for intrigue was incalculable—probably incalculable even to himself. The French Empire was founded. From the Prince on the Masnad to the petty English traders at Madras, the whole of Southern India trembled at the frown of Dupleix. He was the master of thirty millions of men, whom he ruled with more absolute authority than his master ruled the inhabitants of France. If the command of the sea had been assured to him, there is no doubt that the days of the English in India would have been numbered.

Among the causes of the ruin of the French Colonial Empire, the neglect by the home authorities of their brilliant adventurers takes a high place. Dupleix, like all who followed him, suffered severely from this neglect. The empire which he had founded depended, of course, on a kernel of good European troops and a small supply of French officers to train and lead the natives. This would not have been a severe tax on the resources of France—not at all a heavy price to pay for an empire; and, considering the magical consequences of the use to which Dupleix had put the forces actually at his disposal, it may be said to have been absolutely trifling. But he was miserably served in this respect. He ought to have been all the more grateful to Labourdonnais for coming so opportunely to his aid, especially considering that the fleet was provided from Labourdonnais' private resources.

Labourdonnais was Governor of the Isles of France and Bourbon. On the outbreak of war with England he was eager to aid in the expulsion of the English from India. The Government would give him no ships; he managed to get some together himself. If he had no ships, still less had he supplies or men. He managed to provide everything. With a vigour and patriotism that is beyond praise, he made his way with his scratch squadron to the Coromandel coast. He sighted the fleet of Paton, and by feints and a bold bearing that reminds one of the resources of Cochrane he managed to frighten Paton away. He, a retired merchant captain, with an amateur crew, drove off a fleet of King's ships.

He immediately set to work to blockade the town of Madras that Paton had been despatched to guard. Madras capitulated after a bombardment, and was ransomed for a sum variously stated. The average of the different statements is a little over half a million sterling. Here, indeed, was an ally worthy of Dupleix's genius; Dupleix ought to have welcomed him with open arms. He himself, a mere business man, was founding an empire; Labourdonnais, a mere civilian, was capable of beating off a squadron of King's ships, and reducing Madras in less than a week. Two such men, acting together, would have been irresistible.

Dupleix's conduct on this occasion is traceable to no principle of human action except the meanest spite and jealousy, developed to an incomprehensible pitch. Instead of praising Labourdonnais for coming at all, he severely rebuked him for not having come earlier. Instead of warmly thanking him for raising vessels at his own expense, he bitterly complained that his squadron was so weak. He tore up Labourdonnais' treaty, and violated the pledged word of France in the face of all India. Labourdonnais had been literally and emphatically forbidden to make any fresh acquisitions of territory on the mainland; hence his stipulations for a ransom. Dupleix over-rode all his stipulations, burnt Madras to the ground, and carried away the Governor and the principal inhabitants to figure in a sort of triumph at Pondicherry.

It is a miserable exhibition of spite and jealousy from beginning to end, and one stands the more aghast at such a maniacal outbreak in that up to this time one cannot avoid feeling great sympathy with Dupleix. His daring was so great, his genius so original and profound, that we are carried away with admiration for him, in spite of the fact that he was daily compassing the ruin of the English in India.

His jealousy drove Labourdonnais to sea again. Dupleix would concert nothing with the captor of Madras, and the great sailor, who asked nothing better than to serve his country to the best of his ability, was hunted out of the Indian Ocean. Arrived at Mauritius, he found another man, a nominee of Dupleix, installed in his place. His accounts were called for, and he was ordered home. Surely hatred and malice must be exhausted by now.

But Dupleix's fund of jealousy was inexhaustible, and his arm was long. He pursued Labourdonnais to France with his malice, and caused him to be thrown into the Bastile immediately on his arrival in Paris. He was allowed to languish in prison for three years and a half—he, an absolutely innocent man; and not only an innocent man, but one who had rendered the most distinguished services to his country. He was brought out of prison and tried—for what, it would be hard to say. But one reply of his has been preserved, and shows wonderful gallantry and courage, considering his forlorn circumstances. He was asked how it was that his private affairs had prospered so much more than the company's, and he replied to his cross-questioner: 'Because when I managed my own affairs I did what I thought best, and when I had to manage yours I had to do what you told me.'

Labourdonnais was acquitted and set at liberty, but he died six months afterwards of a broken heart. His widow was accorded, with many consoling and flattering expressions, the derisive pension of eight pounds a month.

The fall of Dupleix is generally narrated as if it were the sad fate of a gallant man who is badly supported by his Government, and this is in part true. But the story of the collapse of Dupleix's power is generally told without detailed reference to Labourdonnais, excepting that the two men did not get on well; one's pity is all asked for Dupleix. But when we realize how odiously he behaved to Labourdonnais it is not only without regret, it is with actual complacency that we read the story of his ruin; it is a positive tale of poetic justice.

In Dupleix's situation a navy would have been useful. We have seen how he behaved to the man who brought him one, for no other reason than that the sole merits of its achievements could not be claimed by himself. If a navy was desirable, an army, a European army, was indispensable. Climate and active warfare, and perhaps irregular living, had thinned the ranks of his Frenchmen; his officers were few and incompetent; the recruits sent him were bad material; and Dupleix himself was no soldier. The story told of his preference for an undistinguished position in the rear of a battle, on the ground that the whistling of musket-balls disturbed his reflections, is told on good authority—Dupleix's own. But it is hard to believe that so great a man was a coward. It is incontestable, however, that he was no general.

There was associated with him at this time a young man of considerable military talents, the Marquis de Bussy. Bussy was destined to play towards Lally, in the second great epoch of French adventure, a similar part to that which Labourdonnais played towards Dupleix himself. At this time, however—whether or not it was that he had taken warning by the fate of Labourdonnais—he was far away from headquarters, busily and most successfully engaged in extending French influence in the northern Deccan. The English Dupleix had hitherto, and with good reason, looked down upon as mere book-keepers. The natives thought even more meanly of us.

But among the book-keepers there was a

young man named Robert Clive. It was not Clive who put an end to the ambitions of Dupleix, as we shall see; but he rendered his country this great service, that he changed the English cause from one hopelessly lost into one that had a right to be represented as still existing, and even rivalling the French. For it was in Paris that Dupleix was ruined. If Clive had not, by the defence of Arcot, restored our prestige, and regained for us a party among the natives—in fact, given something for diplomatists to work on, Dupleix would never have been recalled. As it was, we regained by diplomacy most of what had been lost in war.

It was represented by us in Paris that affairs in the East Indies had grown deplorably confused from the habit of French traders interfering in the affairs of native princes. From the English point of view, this was indeed a deplorable habit, for the French were infinitely cleverer at the work than we were. It was further represented that the Governor-General, Dupleix, had greatly exceeded his powers, and that there could be no reasonable expectation of a lasting peace until he was recalled; he was nothing but a fire-brand, so it was urged. These statements were all absolutely true—from the English point of view; but it is none the less extraordinary that the French Ministry should have fallen into so simple a trap. They agreed to desist from interference with native courts; they consented to recall Dupleix. He was recalled, and died in straitened circumstances soon after, of disease brought on by anxiety and disappointment.

His immense fortune had been dissipated in the service of his country, and he could obtain no indemnity for his expenses out of pocket incurred in combating the English. He received no title of honour, and no recognition for his work. Perhaps he sometimes thought of Labourdonnais and his three years of gaol, or, in his poverty, of Madame Labourdonnais, with her pension of eight pounds a month. The fate of both men was a disgrace to their Government, but the fate of Dupleix was, personally, richly deserved.

The first epoch of the great struggle between France and England in India closed on October 5, 1754, when Dupleix sailed from Madras for the last time. His dismissal was a capital blunder on the part of the French Government, but it was only the crowning blunder of a policy of mistakes. These mistakes were: refusing a fleet to Labourdonnais; omitting to censure Dupleix for his treatment of that most useful public servant; permitting Labourdonnais to be iniquitously brought to trial for nobly serving his country; neglecting to send Dupleix a proper supply of soldiers and officers; and finally weakly consenting to his recall.

On all these occasions, we are to remember, it was not a mere possibility that was at stake; the empire was there, already built up. These blunders are all reducible to the single formula: neglect of the Home Government to support its adventurers. Dupleix's only blunder was his atrocious behaviour towards Labourdonnais; he was not too severely punished for it by the neglect that he himself received at the hands of the Home Government.

When we compare the conduct of Dupleix towards Labourdonnais with the conduct of Lawrence towards Clive, we realize that it is actually in a superior moral force that the British found the strength to overthrow the French. Clive had just performed one of the greatest military feats of his generation, and was proceeding on a career of conquest when a superior officer landed. Although Clive had in fact received no military training, his native talent was clearly of the highest order. Yet he at once placed himself under Lawrence's orders. One would say that he did so modestly, if modesty were not altogether out of keeping with his character. In his early days Clive was an extremely ill-bred, ill-mannered young man, sullen to all and insolent to his superiors. In his maturity he showed himself exceedingly vain of a very ugly person, inordinately proud of his peerage and his red ribbon, pushing, ostentatious and assertive. He was fully as acquisitive as Dupleix himself, amassed an immense fortune, and did not conceal the fact that he felt as much pride in his money as in his title. In truth, the mighty Clive was made of very common clay. This haughty, successful, rebellious young man placed himself under the orders of Lawrence—not ostentatiously, boasting of his self-abnegation, but simply and quietly as a matter of duty, or rather as a matter of course.

When we have said thus much it is perhaps unnecessary to add that he did not intrigue against Lawrence, or strive to increase his own glory at the expense of his senior's renown.

If we turn now to Lawrence, we find that he was a deserving, steady officer, a major at that time. He was, as Chesterfield said of Marlborough, 'of a good plain middling understanding,' capable as a soldier, and respectability itself. Respectability is always frightened of genius, and an able, insolent young amateur like Clive was just the sort of man to alarm a Lawrence. He might well, without discredit to himself, have put forward Clive's somewhat irregular position as an excuse for refusing him active employment.

But Lawrence had that touch of loftiness which comes from devotion to one's country, and which can ennoble even the most respectable people. He not only did not decline Clive's services—he not only did not belittle them, or Clive himself—he embraced the chance of availing himself of the services of such a genius of war, a genius so far superior to his own; and he warmly defended Clive against his many enemies who sneered at his 'luck.' 'Not luck,' said Lawrence, 'but eminent ability.'

Here, in a nutshell, is the secret of the downfall of the French Empire in India. Their men were, on the whole, superior to ours, and they had a long start of us. But when it came to a pinch, the English sank all mutual jealousies, and even the most pushing and self-assertive of men felt that there was something at stake greater even than his important self: it was the cause of his country. On the other hand, a crisis was not the moment to choose for inquiring whether Clive's commission came from the Horse-Guards or not. The course of duty was plain—to beat the French; and if Clive could help him, Lawrence was not the man to be jealous of the glory that must of necessity accrue to his subordinate rather than to himself. All this was done without fine phrases, and as a matter of duty, or even as a matter of course.

We have seen how woefully below this standard Dupleix fell. The story of the second great crisis, when for the second time the French Empire was built up, and then torn down by French hands, points the same moral, but points it even more strongly than the story of Dupleix and Labourdonnais. In this epoch we have two great names—

BUSSY—LALLY.

There was a third figure—D'Aché; but although his position as naval commander threw a great deal of power into his hands, and enabled him to do France a vast amount of damage, he was a minor figure altogether, and the story centres round the quarrel between Bussy and Lally.

The Marquis de Bussy—perhaps because

he was a soberer person—has not dazzled the eyes of his countrymen or of the world like the brilliant Dupleix. Nevertheless it may well be argued that he was the greater man. To begin with, he was a good soldier, so his work went on without the friction that everywhere comes from divided command..

He had not Dupleix's unrivalled power of developing and directing secret service, but his own personal ascendancy was very great. He was a much simpler character than Dupleix. He did not indulge in fanfares or displays, but he made up for this loss of power—a real loss of power in the East—by the solid advantage that he gained from his directness of character. The native princes came to lean on him and look up to him, and though he never called himself a Rájá, his influence was immense.

His sphere of action was the Deccan, his centre the Imperial city of Aurangabad. It is perhaps significant that this was a conveniently long way from Dupleix. His influence was at its height in the year 1754, at which date he was thirty-six years of age, and we have thus to realize that at the moment when Dupleix was recalled, the French Empire in India almost extended over the whole of Southern India. Dupleix's empire, somewhat damaged by the assault of Clive, was reduced to possession; Bussy's needed only the touch of a small and competent military force to transform it from a sphere of influence into a grand dominion.

Owing either to indifference, or else (which is less easy to believe) to extreme gullibility, the French ministry had played our game with a thoroughness and promptitude that we could not have desired to see exceeded, and had recalled Dupleix, leaving no successor. There remained, however, Bussy. The French Government appears to have realized when too late that they had acted with something less than wisdom, and were already repenting their precipitate recall of Dupleix when the Seven Years' War broke out. They determined to seize the opportunity and to regain by vigorous military action what had been taken from them by able negotiation.

It was a very good opening. Clive was in Europe; Bussy's influence in the Deccan was extending daily; the English had just been expelled from Bengal, so that nothing remained of the British Empire in the East but the feeble settlements on the Coromandel coast. To Bussy's mind these settlements did not greatly matter one way or the other. If his own plan succeeded, and he formed a great French inland State, it would be a State of such dimensions that it would be independent of the command of the sea; if the English became troublesome they could always be expelled without any great difficulty. He looked forward eagerly to the arrival of an army from Europe, hoping to engage the commandant (whoever he might prove to be) in his plans.

The officer selected for the command was Thomas Arthur Lally, at that time one of the greatest living masters of regular warfare. He had been aide-de-camp to Prince Charlie in the '45. Wherever there had been an opportunity of striking a blow at England, Lally had been foremost—he had struck us hard at Fontenoy with his brigade of Irish: hatred to England was the inspiration of his career. A special regiment of Irish had been raised for him, and the command of it conferred on him. He was created Baron of Tollendal and Count of Lally, and advanced to the dignity of a Grand Cross of St. Louis. When he took up the Indian command, he was fifty-three years of age.

The first comment that occurs to us on this appointment is, that Lally was too great a man for the place. It was also remarked, at the time, with some misgiving, that Lally had had no experience of irregular warfare, and was known to be a strict disciplinarian. To both of these reasonings a sufficient answer was found; Lally was no doubt a man of considerable position, holding the rank of a full Lieutenant-General, among other distinctions; but that only showed how much importance the Government attached to the conquest of India. It was true that he was a stern soldier, but then he was to take his own regiment of Irish, 1,080 strong, with him, and they were accustomed to his ways. We shall see how far this reasoning was sound, and what other points there were that the minister had not, perhaps, sufficiently weighed, before selecting Lally. It is easy to be wise after the event; but the wisest course would have been to send Bussy the men. But Bussy was a company's officer, and the Government was uneasy at the idea of having a second Dupleix on their hands. So Lally was despatched, and the idea that an Irish refugee, commanding his own regiment of Irishmen, was about to dash in pieces the fabric of what remained of the British Empire in India, naturally threw over the expedition a sort of halo of retributive justice.

On April 28, 1758, four years after the death of Dupleix, seven years after the death of Labourdonnais, Lally landed at Pondicherry. The actors in the first great drama had passed away, with the exception of Bussy, who (properly supported) might yet have retrieved everything. But Lally paid no attention to him. Moreover, we are to remark that Lally came a little late. When the Seven Years' War broke out, the English were expelled from Bengal, and if Lally had reduced the settlements on the Coromandel, he could have come to the assistance of the enemies of England in Bengal, and crossed swords with Clive there. But in 1758 we had regained our old position, and greatly increased our authority. Clive had fought Plassy, and Coote was with him, already soon to be—at thirty-three—a Lieutenant-Colonel. Lally's task was, at least, doubled.

He turned first to the easy task of reducing the Madras Settlements, and it now appeared that he was hopelessly out of place in his Indian command. Obviously, his first duty was to get the settlement into something like order, to expel the English, and consolidate his forces to resist the attack that was to be expected from Bengal. To achieve this much, the mere commencement of his work, he would need the hearty co-operation of all alike—French and native. By way of compassing this end, he denounced the French as a pack of swindlers, and the natives as black swine. It is true that his instructions contained some reference to peculation which Lally was to put down, but he chose the most inopportune moment to disclose his instructions, and abuse, which is always useless, was at this juncture simply disastrous.

There have always been capable men who can do eminently good work if the service runs on wheels, but who are disconcerted at the first break-down in commissariat or transport. Lally was one of these. His native temper disqualified him for compromise. He was bitter and imperious. The habits of a lifetime had made him a master of regular warfare, but his mind was stiff with age, and he became more and more irritable as difficulties multiplied, and his own helplessness in the face of them became daily more apparent. Transport failed, so he pressed all the natives, irrespective of caste, into the transport service, thus ruining in a week the work of half a century of intelligent handling of the natives. Money ran short, so he called on Bussy to supply him out of the hoards that he at once presumed him to have accumulated after the fashion of Dupleix. In point of fact Bussy was not an acquisitive man, and he received Lally's demand with a simplicity that only an innocent man, or a most accomplished rogue, could assume. Lally favoured him in return with so insulting a stare that Bussy was mortally affronted.

Bussy was the man on whom Lally ought to have leant with absolute confidence; he possessed tact, of which Lally was totally destitute; local information, which Lally neither possessed nor attempted to acquire; and immense influence. He had hurried down from Aurangabad to greet Lally on his arrival, and to engage his interest in his plans. These plans were to carry the newly-landed troops inland, and away from the Coromandel coast (which would be good for their health) to engage them in the task of converting the Deccan 'sphere of influence' into a dominion, and to allow the English (if they dared—which they certainly would not) to attack the French in their inland stronghold. Lally pooh-poohed Bussy's ideas, not only with contempt, but with insult. 'It is already too much condescension to listen to the vapourings of that madman,' he wrote.

A man must be very confident indeed of his own ability before he can use such strong language about a colleague's views. But when we learn what Lally's own plans were, we can only conclude that if anybody was mad it certainly was not Bussy. 'It is in Bengal that we must strike at the English,' he wrote; 'I shall proceed to the Ganges by sea or land, and it is there that I shall find your talents and experience of great use to me.'

From Madras to the Ganges by land! with an army of five hundred Frenchmen and a few discontented native troops, without money, without transport, and without supplies! It is the dream of a lunatic or a very ignorant man. Perhaps by sea then? It seems incredible, but it is nevertheless the fact that when Lally talked about proceeding to Bengal by sea he actually had no fleet, D'Aché having sailed away, after a slight brush with the English, in September, 1758.

Lally had landed on the Coromandel coast in April, 1757. It was not till November, 1759, that he met Coote in battle. During that period of two years and six months, he might, if he had listened to Bussy, have turned the whole of the Deccan into so great a military state, that he could have crushed the English settlements by the dead weight of the French impact, just as the English had ousted the French in Canada. Instead, he had gained trifling victories and undergone trifling reverses; he had destroyed the native confidence in the French, and ruined Bussy's schemes. With the remains of his discontented army he had now to fight as great a soldier as himself—Eyre Coote.

Sir Eyre Coote was born in the year 1726; he had been with Clive at Plassy, and was just created Lieutenant-Colonel. His experience in warfare was entirely Indian, and, therefore, although Lally's junior by twenty-four years, he was a more competent general for campaigning on the Coromandel coast than the unfortunate Frenchman.

It is not too much to say that his Sepoys

adored him, whereas Lally's troops may have feared their chief; but they also regarded him with some suspicion and more dislike. On November 30, 1759, Coote gained the great victory of Wandewash; on the 22nd of the succeeding January he defeated Lally and took Bussy prisoner. On January 5, 1761, he captured Pondicherry and took Lally himself prisoner. For the second time the French Empire in India was broken down. But the second collapse was far more serious than the first. Dupleix's empire had been destroyed by dexterously securing his recall, and when he retired the English were left with no great authority in India; in fact, they were still very little respected as soldiers. But Bussy's empire, so far as the natives could see, had fallen in a way that they could understand; it had gone down before the assault of Coote. Henceforth it is the English who stand forth as the martial race. Of course, that is only half the story, and there is no doubt that if Lally (who was quite as good a soldier as Coote) had pulled with Bussy instead of ignorantly spurning his help, the result would have been entirely different.

Lally's fate is generally cited as a shocking example of the ingratitude of kings. It is terrible to be guillotined for an error of judgment, but, then, what a gigantic error it was! Moreover, it was not an error committed, like Byng's, in a moment of battle; it was persisted in for two years and a half, during all of which time it must have been perfectly plain to Lally himself, without consulting Bussy or anybody else, that the French cause in his hands was going from bad to worse. He certainly deserved severe punishment; it would hardly have been too severe treatment if he had been broken and dismissed the service. His fate depended a good deal on the attitude of Bussy. The Marquis's intentions were very plainly expressed in five words—
'Either Lally's head or mine,' he said.

It was almost too much to expect that Bussy should show himself a generous enemy. His noble ambitions were ruined in the moment of fruition, his glorious dreams dissipated, himself defeated and a prisoner of war. From the moment that the French cause was ruined he set himself to work to glut his revenge on Lally. The unhappy General came to England and was warmly received. He was our determined foe, and had been so all his life; but he had always been a gallant foe, and he was now, in the autumn of his days, a most unfortunate man. Bussy went straight to Paris. He was connected by marriage with Choiseul the Minister, and Choiseul gave Lally a friendly hint that he would do well to stay out of France for a time. Lally's English friends did their best to keep him in London, but he brushed all remonstrances aside, and betook himself to Paris to demand a trial. His prosecution was commenced on July 6, 1763, and was fiercely pushed on. On May 5, 1766, he was condemned to death, and on May 9, Thomas Arthur, Baron of Tollendal, Count of Lally, a Knight Grand Cross of the Order of St. Louis, and Lieutenant-General, being now sixty-four years of age, was dragged through Paris on a hurdle, with a gag in his mouth, and guillotined.

Bussy's revenge was now glutted; perhaps we may not blame him; perhaps Lally deserved his fate — or very nearly deserved it. Nevertheless, these fierce personal animosities have much to answer for in the ruin of the cause of the French Indian Empire. The first of these gorgeous fabrics was built up by Dupleix, and by Dupleix it was ruined out of jealousy of Labourdonnais. The second was built up by Bussy, and ruined by Lally out of jealousy of Bussy. The third never got further than the foundations, its erection being suddenly arrested by the conclusion of peace. The year 1763 saw the conclusion of the Treaty of Paris. By that Treaty France lost Canada, and prior to its conclusion she had suffered very heavy losses in India; concurrently with these losses by France immense additional territories had been acquired by England in Bengal.

It is not to be expected that a great nation, proud and mighty, like France, should tamely endure such intolerable humiliation. Peace was no sooner concluded than her Ministers were at work in every direction for a new attack on England. Although by a strange contrast the English Ministries remained for long after the Treaty of Paris feeble and frivolous, in one direction we were active—secret service. Very curious it is to read the record of mining and counter-mining that went on about that period, our agents working hard to discover Choiseul's plans, while Choiseul carefully put forward misleading plans, which were eagerly transmitted to London as proof of the zeal and acumen of our agents.

The French had learnt one great lesson from the Seven Years' War: they must not engage at one and the same time in hostilities on the Continent and in a naval campaign with Great Britain. Accordingly, their continental relations were kept peaceable, while their navy was steadily increased in strength and improved in quality.

In England, as the French saw with pleasure, each Government was feebler and more incompetent than its predecessor. France was watchfully biding her time.

The rebellion of the American colonies gave her her chance, and we have seen how she availed herself of it. When things were going sufficiently ill for England in the West, when it seemed as if the sun of England's glory was really setting, France planned a grand attack on the British Empire in the East.

Her diplomatic activity there had never ceased, and in Haidar she found a lever for overthrowing the English ready to her hand. Her plan now was to stir up this mighty soldier to overthrow the English, and, without attempting land operations on a grand scale on her own account, to cut the English off from obtaining succour by sea by means of a powerful French squadron in the Indian Ocean. An admirable plan, and it was admirably carried out, and had actually succeeded, when the Treaty of Versailles snatched away the third and last chance that fell to France of founding a great Indian Empire. The man selected for the naval part of the work was the greatest sailor of France, and perhaps the second greatest sailor that ever lived—Bailli Suffren.

The parallel between Suffren and Nelson is inevitable. Both were extremely nervous, irritable, excitable, and anxious men, but the ways in which their tempers manifested themselves were very different, and were derived from the training of their lives. Nelson was of humble extraction, and raised himself to great eminence. In the course of his rise he had to practise, as a chief element of his success, the greatest self-command and even self-repression. Suffren was a great French noble, accustomed all his life to deference as his due and obedience as his right. One consequence of Nelson's training was that he suffered from fits of profound depression; his anxiety ran to melancholy and even hysteria. Suffren's anxiety exploded in outbursts of fury, or boiled over in torrents of scalding invective.

These contrary results reacted on their subordinates, and on the crews under their command, which were from the outset crews and officers of a very different stamp. Nelson's crews had been moulded by the iron will of St. Vincent and Howe into a state of perfect discipline; his officers were mostly men like himself. The consequence was that when Nelson took command they followed him to battle not only with readiness, but with rapture. Suffren's captains were also men like unto himself—indolent, haughty nobles, and their Admiral's temper did not tend to weld them together.

Nelson was lean to emaciation, but of an infinitely kind and winning temper, and not so careful of his dignity that he minded 'shinning' up the rigging to show a trembling middy, newly come aboard, that there was nothing to be frightened of in going aloft.

Suffren was enormously fat and choleric, and as much of a grand seigneur on his quarter-deck as on his *terres*. Nelson's sphere of action was much grander than Suffren's, and the consequence of all these contrary conditions is that, while Nelson appears in history as a ruler of the battle and the tempest, a very god of war, who, when he smote his enemies, not only defeated but destroyed them, Suffren is to most of us a name only. Nelson was dead at forty-seven; Suffren was ten years older before he fought his great battles.

There may be a question which of the two was the greater sailor, the greater master of tactics and resource; but when we read how Suffren's laggard captains betrayed him over and over again, there can be no doubt which was the greater man.

The English Admiral opposed to Suffren was Sir Edward Hughes, a good specimen of an English sailor, who generally gets less credit than his due, because in his last encounter with Suffren, having eighteen sail to Suffren's fifteen, he declined a decisive battle. He is supposed to have lost his nerve. But seeing that this was his fifth fleet action with Suffren in the course of two years, the wonder is not so much that he lost his nerve, but that he had not lost it earlier. To have fought four fleet actions with Suffren, and not to be utterly defeated, is enough glory for one man.

Suffren arrived off the coast of Coromandel with an inferior fleet, and, although not uniformly victorious, he yet continually improved his position. He had no base originally; he supplied his want by conquering one—Trincomalee. He had no spare yards or rigging; he got them partly from captured prizes, partly by improvising them from material obtained ashore. He was a complete master of the art of developing resources out of nothing. He was granted only a small fraction of the military support that had been promised by France to Haidar; nevertheless, by diplomatic treatment he contrived to keep that chieftain in fighting mood.

As regards the land operations, he had but little responsibility; they were entrusted to Bussy, now a gouty invalid of sixty-four. But Bussy was no match for Coote, who was now fifty-three years of age, and a K.B. He had been appointed Commander-in-Chief in India in 1777, and took up his command on March 25, 1779. He took the field in Madras very unwillingly, being in feeble health; but in July, 1781, he gained the great victory of Porto Novo, and continued victorious throughout the years 1781 and 1782. In the next year he died. Bussy survived him till 1785, when he died at Pondicherry.

But after Porto Novo there was little chance of making great progress on land. Everything depended on Suffren. If Hughes' fleet could be destroyed, the English settlements would be cut off and compelled to surrender. Suffren, like all the great French Imperial pioneers, was badly served by the Home Government. Instead of sending him reinforcements of sufficient strength to reach the East, ships were forwarded by twos and threes. These little companies were not strong enough to force their way unharmed through the narrow seas; often they were cut off; often when they reached Suffren they did so with forces impaired by conflict. But Suffren's genius supplied all defects. Hughes seems to have fought with him in something of Wellington's spirit: 'It was not for me to bandy manœuvres with the greatest captain of the age; all that

I had to do was to stand still and resist him.'

'What am I to do with the ship, sir?' said the sailing master of one of Hughes' captains, when he had an overwhelming strength bearing down on the ship. 'There is nothing to be done with her,' said the captain, 'except to fight her till she sinks.'

It was in this temper that the English fought; they were in the grip of a commanding genius, but they prolonged the struggle for years. At last Suffren had achieved his end. He was blockading Madras, where our feeble forces were surrounded on the land side. Hughes was cruising outside Suffren's fleet, but he dared not close with that terrible foe. His nerve failed him, and he sailed away. The fall of Madras was imminent, and with Madras would have gone the ascendancy over the whole of Southern India. On June 29 there came a messenger with a white flag, bearing the news that the Treaty of Versailles had been signed on February 9 preceding. So passed away the last great danger to India from the French.

Suffren was neither guillotined for his services nor banished to his estates; he was received with the most distinguished honour at Versailles. But what gratified him even more than his honour in France was the attention that he received from the English. His own captains did not appreciate him. The long campaign had irritated and fatigued them. They had little interest in the object of their labours, and they were exhausted by Suffren's endless activity, and had no eye for his genius.

But the English captains crowded to see him, to have the honour of shaking hands with so great a master of their craft, to be face to face with the great sailor before whose mighty assault even their stout hearts had so often stood still. With the roar of Suffren's broadsides yet in their ears, our captains pressed on board his flagship, to pay homage to the greatest Admiral of history— the man who was greater than De Ruyter, than Rooke, or Hawke himself. His own captains had no homage to offer except the homage of a grudging obedience.

The interposition of the Treaty of Versailles was a piece of sheer good luck. We had fought stoutly, but we must needs have gone under if war had continued. Haidar was dead, it is true; but then so was Coote. The navy dominated the situation, and Suffren had won his campaign.

It is hard to say whether we ought to include in the Lost Empire of France those territories that she gained by the annexation of Holland. When the Emperor Napoleon raised his brother Louis to the throne of Holland the latter country became a tributary of France, and the Dutch colonial possessions were engulfed in the huge extent of the Empire. They included the Cape of Good Hope and Java. Both were captured by English troops: the first by an expedition under Sir David Bain, sent out from England; the second by an expedition under Sir Samuel Auchmuty, sent out from India. Java was restored and the Cape of Good Hope retained.

Of course, immense and sudden accretions of strength like these will always follow in the wake of a prodigious military force, wielded by a genius like Napoleon. Even these triumphs are nothing to what he effected in Europe itself; but there is no lesson to be drawn from these events, except the very primitive one that the strong will always conquer the weak. Spain once enjoyed an empire in Europe of the same kind, an empire founded partly on superior military forces; but also owing its immense extent, very largely, to a long series of lucky marriages of her princes to heiresses of great territories. But this also is not the kind of empire that is valuable as a study for Englishmen, seeking light from history on their own performances.

The Lost Empire of France, in so far as it was an empire, such as England at present holds, was lost to France for reasons which have been examined as shortly as possible in these pages. France possessed a very large number of those valuable and, indeed, indispensable pioneers—adventurers.

One colony, Canada, was strong and flourishing, even although very few settlers followed in the wake of the great Canadian adventurers. The colony founded by adventure, and strengthened by a very small infusion of colonizing blood, was more than a match for the English settlements, thickly populated in comparison though they were.

It went down, not before the New England settlers, but before the sheer dead weight of the English assault. It was a colony with its roots already struck deep into the ground; adequately supported from France, it would have grown to dominate the continent. In India the adventurers had full play. There it was the personal rivalry that ruined the French cause. Dupleix quarrelled with Labourdonnais; Lally quarrelled with Bussy.

On the whole, we must conclude that adventure was the driving force, East and West, of France: in the West adventure was not supported by the Home Government; in the East adventure did brilliantly; it was not so much from lack of support that its achievements melted away, it was on account of the mutual jealousies of the adventurers.

We must note, however, that on the one occasion when there was nobody to be jealous of, France got the upper hand completely, thanks to the genius of Suffren; and here, too, as in Canada, a little help from France would have turned the scale before the Treaty of Versailles robbed France of the fruits of her efforts.

In the West Indies it is now, as then and always, simply the superior naval power that dominates. In Africa France has not only lost nothing, she has very largely increased the area of her influence and authority. It is there that (as we saw from the passage of M. Leroy Beaulieu quoted at the head of this chapter) France hopes yet to redeem the losses of the past by founding a great African Empire.

Whether she will do so or not depends simply on the two questions: firstly, Can she induce her people to multiply and colonize, wherever colonization is possible? and, secondly, Will she make up her mind to adequately support her adventurers, and to prevent them from quarrelling with each other?

V.

THE LOST EMPIRE OF HOLLAND.

V.

THE LOST EMPIRE OF HOLLAND.

THE Dutch Empire holds our attention (not always our admiring attention) from the moment of its rise down to the present day. Its history is a long series of surprises, beginning with its origin, which seemed the most unlikely thing in the world, and continuing for two centuries and a half down to the date when, in defiance of all accepted conclusions, a very small country continues to occupy a very large position in the eyes of the world.

It is also fairly open to argument that the Dutch Empire should have no place in this volume because it is not lost. It still includes the island of Java, a great part of Borneo, New Guinea, practically the whole of Sumatra, the Celebes, and the Moluccas—all of which, taken together, imply the dominion of the East Indian Archipelago. It also includes, in the West Indies, the island of Curaçao, and some dependencies. Great and even grandiose as these present possessions are for so small a State, the Lost Empire of Holland is yet of sufficient magnitude to justify the inclusion in this volume of an examination of the whole. It includes chiefly 'possibilities' —the possibility of a great North American State, expanding from the very early settlement of New Amsterdam; the possibility of a great South African State, expanding from the settlement of the Cape of Good Hope; the possibility of a great Indian Empire, arising from the Dutch settlements on the Ganges and the island of Ceylon. It includes also a few important posts, and much ill-defined but once lucrative 'influence' on the West Coast of Africa, where Holland, like most of the European nations, has scrambled for a trade which was variously described as ivory, gum, or gold, but which was always and substantially slaves.

The Dutch are not a decadent nation; on the contrary, they are probably as vigorous at the present moment as they ever were. But they do not owe the retention of their imperial position to their superior vitality: they owe it to the unexampled condescension of Great Britain; for the entire area of the present Dutch Empire has been twice conquered by England, and twice handed back to Holland. The reasons for this self-denial on our part will be given later.

If the empire of Portugal was a triumph of thought, that of Spain an empire of plunder and slaughter after the Oriental model, that of France a triumph of brilliant adventure, the empire of Holland has also its distinguishing characteristic—it is a miracle of shopkeeping. In its history we find no principles appealed to or applied that are beyond the range of the humblest linen-draper's intelligence. There are no striking figures in Dutch colonial history; the whole nation went as one firm into the business of empire as they might have gone into any other trade. They succeeded, and amassed in that important trade immense wealth. But it is chiefly in their exclusive addiction to earning large returns on the capital embarked, and to their consequent neglect of the natives whom they exploited to their profit, that we shall find whatever grounds for reprehension there may be in the history of the empire of Holland.

First, of its rise. The sixteenth century found the Dutch a thrifty and thriving folk, living well among their dykes, in spite of all the hardships of their climate. They prosecuted a busy trade and cultivated the domestic virtues. They were not a very adventurous race, and not at all an imaginative. In commerce they delighted in quick returns and large profits; they were content, under protest, with small profits, but the returns must be quick. They were very good traders on commission, and quickly absorbed almost the whole of the distributing business of the wealthy empire of Portugal. They had not the distinct national existence that they have now, and have had for some centuries past, their mother-country being only a part of the

Low Countries, and each State semi-independent, like those of the Swiss. The basis of their character was a steady, not to say stubborn, conservatism, and a loyalty to their rulers that ranked next only after religious conviction.

No race more unlikely to embark on the dangerous, the exciting, but eminently gambling, business of empire-making could possibly be imagined. What force, one might well ask, could possibly stimulate such a people to embark on the race in which Portugal and Spain (such very different countries from Holland) had up to the rise of the Dutch Empire won all the prizes?

We know from Mr. Motley's works how tremendous was the force applied to mould the Dutch into a nation—a nation not only separate, but adventurous and belligerent. It required nothing less than the scourge of Philip's tyranny to move them. This solid and stolid people, who asked nothing better than to remain for ever the most loyal and devoted of Philip's subjects, found themselves under the necessity of choosing between submission (which meant extinction) and conquest (which implied empire, if they chose to snatch the prize).

The quarrel of course was religious. These heretics (or assertors of the rights of conscience, whichever phrase you will), stung by the scorpion lash of Alva's intolerable despotism, sprang at their master's throat. This 'people of butter'—as Alva in his Spanish pride and Turkish ignorance had called them—flung off the yoke of Spain, conquered her, trampled on her, and despoiled her, and built up for themselves a wealthy and stable empire out of her depredations. Wealthy and stable: these are words to conjure with, with Dutchmen. It was not gorgeous, it was not imposing. It was so little magnificent, that its very existence is often at the present day overlooked; but it was and is, even in its shorn condition, eminently remunerative.

Such, then, are, in brief, the conditions under which the empire of Holland took its rise. It was conceived in rebellion and nourished on piracy—noble rebellion and justifiable piracy, if you will, but still rebellion and piracy. That it should have arisen at all is remarkable ; but the direction in which Holland expanded, and the character of her imperial work, are alike hardly less remarkable.

The rebellion was against Spain, the piracy was directed against Spain ; but it was so directed, without apparent rancour or bitterness, and in a discriminating and (so to speak) methodical manner, that is in every way exceptional.

When the Dutch Empire took its rise, the whole known world outside Europe was in Spanish hands. The original Spanish Empire had been of immense extent, but had been entirely confined to the Western Hemisphere (with the trifling exception of the small Spanish acquisitions in the South Seas). Since the year 1580, however, it had been doubled in extent by the absorption of the whole Portuguese Empire into the empire of Spain, and the Portugo-Spanish Empire thus added included the whole of the known East —the known East added to the known West made a universal empire on which the Dutch might prey at will. 'The world was all before them where to choose.'

It is true that there remained over and above the extent of the Spanish and the Portugo-Spanish Empire the whole continent of North America. In exploiting and exploring this immense and unknown territory, France and England were at this moment throwing off their first crop of adventurers. Experiments were almost yearly being made by both nations; but experiments were not much in the Dutchman's way, still less adventure.

If he was to cross the ocean and risk his life by sea and in unknown lands, it would not be in search of adventure or that he might make experiments. He did, indeed, as we shall see, make one settlement on the Atlantic coast; but, in the modern phrase, 'there was no money' in North America. The same sagacious, if not very lofty, instinct that deterred him from experiments in the North American continent also overcrowded any natural desire that he may have had to wreak his vengeance on Spain by directing his piracies on the old Spanish Empire in Central and Southern America. The Spanish Empire was essentially military, and though the Hollanders did not shrink from fights when they were unavoidable, they preferred spheres of action that were peaceful as well as profitable. Moreover, the profits of the Spanish Empire were precarious. Looting is an affair of hours, and all the loot of Mexico and Peru had long since been collected and spent. There remained the mines—profitable indeed, but essentially gambling securities. The Dutch turned aside from the original Spanish Empire of the West towards the Portugo-Spanish Empire of the East.

Beyond the fact that both these extensive empires were now subject to the Crown of Spain, there had been no attempt to amalgamate them, or to fuse interests that had from the commencement been kept rigidly distinct. Portugal and Spain, both religious nations, had scrupulously observed the Papal award which gave the East to one and the West to the other. Even for purposes of convenience, Spain made no attempt (while the empires were still distinct) to intrude on her neighbour's territory. Slaves, for example, were necessary to her for the development of her American estates; but she did not attempt to acquire, either by purchase, settlement, or conquest, any posts on the West Coast of Africa to serve as bases for a slave supply. She left the lucrative business of supplying America with blacks entirely in the hands of the Portuguese—in obedience to the Papal award.

This was just the kind of trade that attracted the Dutch, and we accordingly find them settled on the rock of Goree, off the West Coast of Africa, between the Senegal and the Gambia, as early as the year 1617. Another yet more lucrative, and much less dangerous, trade was that of the Spice Islands, on which Holland had long cast envious eyes. The goods were of small bulk and very precious, owing to the limited supply. Both spice trade and slave trade were, of course, in the hands of the Portuguese, and must be acquired by force. Moreover, the spice trade implied the possession of islands at the uttermost parts of the earth. Naval superiority was, therefore, the first indispensable condition for the absorption of the Portuguese Empire by Holland. How great that naval superiority rapidly became we shall presently see; but in the meantime we may note that the Dutch Empire had none of the characteristics that we should have expected it to possess when we reflect on the sinister circumstances attending its origin.

Considering that the Dutch had only just emerged from the hellish ordeal of Philip's tyranny, we should expect to find them burning with violent and disorderly passions. If they were capable of any great constructive effort we should expect to find their empire taking the shape of a series of strong naval stations from which they could swoop down and plunder their enemies. This was not at all what happened. They emerged from their great trials almost unaltered in character, and they promptly and methodically set to work to build up a great trading empire, apparently almost uninfluenced by considerations of revenge.

They started with many advantages. The Portuguese, who could fight stoutly enough for themselves, fought but languidly for a foreign master, and they had recently succumbed to the same tyranny that Holland had just thrown off. The Portuguese were depressed; the Dutch flushed with their successful resistance to Spain. Moreover, the Dutch were much better sailors. The early trade to the East had been carried on in very large slow-sailing ships. There were good reasons for this; the long voyage, with uncertain ports of call, necessitated careful provisioning, and large crews must be carried to meet the accident of a fight. The Portuguese had made very little progress in naval architecture, and they were at the mercy of the Dutch.

The Dutch have followed somewhat in the wake of the Portuguese in this matter. We can still—on the rare occasions when a Dutchman sails through the Downs—study the type of vessel with which Holland fought her way to the Spice Islands two centuries and more ago. It is difficult to realize that these leisurely if eminently seaworthy craft, whose lines have hardly changed since the days of Van Tromp, were in the days of the rise of the Dutch Empire the smartest ships afloat.

When the Dutch turned their thoughts eastwards it was in vessels not much heavier and slower than these that they sailed. At that time they were in the forefront of progress in the matter of naval architecture, for they had been fighting for a whole generation in the narrow seas where handiness was everything, and fighting for national existence. Consequently, when little fleets of vessels like this fell in with a Portuguese galleon, the Portuguese had no chance; it was the Armada over again on a small scale wherever Portuguese and Dutch came into collision.

These, then, are the conditions under which the Dutch Empire developed. They had a decided naval superiority, and the enemy in occupation of the wealthiest portion of the earth's surface was feeble and dispirited. There was no discovery to be done; for by the time that the Dutch entered on their Imperial career the road to the East, and even the Far East, was almost a beaten track. There is very little individual enterprise to be recorded, and the Dutch owe next to nothing to that source of strength; the whole nation marched, so to speak, along the road eastward to the Spice Islands.

They established themselves at Goree; they settled at the Cape of Good Hope; they ousted the Portuguese from Ceylon; they threw off side settlements in the Indian Peninsula; and they expelled the Portuguese from the whole of the wealthy archipelago, known as the Spice Islands.

Thus the shape that the Dutch Empire takes at its height is this: there is a large group of possessions—Java, the Moluccas, the Celebes, Malacca—where the natives were not formidable, where a small garrison could hold each island or group with ease, and where each could come to the help of a neighbour when threatened. This group is strong, as well as compact. It is situated at the farthest extremity of the earth's surface from Europe, and can, consequently, only be attacked by a powerful naval expedition. Such an expedition must be prepared to fight every stage of the voyage, or else be prepared to sail the 12,000 miles without putting in anywhere; for all the ports of call are in Dutch hands, and firmly held—Goree, the Cape, Ceylon. This is a very strongly cemented chain of possessions, and its commercial value was simply what the Dutch chose to make it; for the produce of the Far East was grown nowhere else, and the whole of the Far East was Dutch.

It was not a dangerous exploit, for the Portuguese were not vigorous opponents. It was not an adventurous exploit, for the road was clear and well marked out before the Dutch entered on it. It was a rich prize easily won, and over the whole there hangs a certain flavour of the commonplace, which is hardly, perhaps, to be wondered at when we come to consider the way in which the Dutch looked on their newly-won dominions, and the manner in which they exploited them. But we must not underrate it. It was, no doubt, a remarkable achievement for so small a people. It will appear still more worthy of attention when we quit the task of narrating where and how the Dutch displaced their predecessors, and enter on an examination of some of the circumstances that attended their expansion of Holland.

There were, as we have seen, no difficulties of the kind encountered by Portugal and Spain ; difficulties of discovery, or the difficulty of dealing with powerful native kingdoms already established in the lands to be acquired. Had the Dutch, then, no difficulties to face?

They had difficulties and great ones ; but their difficulties were quite different from any experienced by the Portuguese or Spanish, and arose entirely in consequence of the Dutch entering so late on their career of expansion.

The Portuguese and Spaniards explored at their ease. They had no rivals, and so they had time to make mistakes and profit by them, to remedy their blunders, and to begin again. But the Dutch had no sooner started than France and England were close on their heels.

Thus, although Holland commenced to lay the foundations of a Colonial Empire at one and the same time in North America, in the West India Islands, on the West Coast of Africa, in the continent of India, and in the Far East, she was quickly compelled to give up most of these enterprises by the encroachments of her neighbours. It was not that the individual Dutchman was in any way the inferior of the individual Frenchman or Englishman; it was simply that there were not in the aggregate enough Dutchmen to hold all these posts.

Considering their numbers the Dutch made a wonderful impression of universal empire. This was because they had no desire for conquest for conquest's sake—no ideal loftier than the enrichment of Dutchmen. If they had wasted their strength in attempting the conquest of India or Brazil they would rapidly have sunk to the position of an insignificant European Power, without any external relations worth mentioning. But they attempted no such Quixotic enterprises, and the consequence was that they made such a show of strength that France and England were only too thankful to leave to the Dutch the trade of the Far East, provided that they could acquire some share of the trade of the rest of the world.

For it so happened that the kind of trade that the Dutch monopolized was just that which most aroused the jealousy and covetousness of both France and England—the carrying trade.

Just as, while their trade was confined to Europe, the Dutch had become the great distributors of the Continent, so when they entered on their career of imperial expansion they aimed at, and in fact conquered, the carrying trade of the ocean.

But just as the prudent investor buys, in times of peace, shares in a small-arms manufactory, so the Dutch, foreseeing perhaps the jealousy that their predominance in the carrying trade would arouse, set themselves from the outset to make a second string to their bow. This was their trade with the Far East, of which they had, from the commencement of their successful assaults on the Portugo-Spanish Empire, the exclusive monopoly.

This trade it was that remained longest in the hands of the Dutch, this empire it was that was twice conquered and twice restored by England. The other possessions of Holland, which were snatched from her comparatively early, were posts established by her for the sake of the convenience of her carrying trade.

It was in defending these latter outposts that the weakness of Holland, in point of numbers, became so grievously apparent.

By far the most famous of all, the most wealthy potentially and the most interesting, was the settlement on the Atlantic coast known as New Amsterdam. In this part of the continent there were, in those days, no opportunities of acquiring wealth rapidly. In Africa the natives, if savages, were at any rate savages with whom a profitable trade could be carried on. In North America the case was different. Those precious goods of small bulk—ivory, gold, gum, spices—that so attracted the Dutchman were not to be had. The slow processes of agriculture, and (while the population remained scanty) still slower processes of petty commerce, were the only roads to wealth. For these reasons comparatively few Dutchmen went there. No very powerful military establishment was kept up. There was, therefore, nothing to counterbalance the very great advantages that a naturally prolific and pushing race would have over one more conservative and of fewer numbers. The English, French and Dutch were all early established on the mainland of North America; but whereas the French, from their greater numbers (and also from their being separated from the English by a natural boundary) long disputed the domination of the continent with the English, the Dutch were, from the outset, in a much more unfavourable situation.

Their colony of New Amsterdam was hemmed in by English settlements. After half a century of European immigration, the Dutch population was probably not one-seventh of the English. Plainly so great a disparity of forces could end in but one way at the first outbreak of hostilities.

It was only in the forbearance of the English that the Dutch could look for a long continuance of their own power.

Towards the middle of the seventeenth century the English, so far from feeling indulgently towards the Dutch, were intensely jealous of them on account of their predominance in the carrying trade. To this feeling we owe the Navigation Laws of Cromwell and the Dutch Wars of Charles II. It was in the year 1664 that the nascent Dutch Empire in North America was destroyed at a single blow, and the colony of New Amsterdam converted into the colony of New York.

A far more serious blow befell her, at about the same time, in the loss of the slave trade dependent on her station of Goree on the West Coast of Africa.

This trade, as we have seen, was carried

on by the Portuguese, and the Spaniards made no attempts to snatch at it. Even when the Portuguese were ousted by the Dutch, and the Spaniards found themselves, in consequence, face to face with the necessity of choosing between slaves purveyed by rebels and heretics or no slaves at all, they acquiesced peacefully in the transfer; either out of continued respect for the Papal award, or from native sluggishness, or from the tardy conviction that the Dutch were more than a match for them. This trade, then, passed into Dutch hands. They supplied their own small settlements in Guiana and the Brazils with slaves, and they also supplied the Spaniards. With Goree—lost first to the English and recovered from them, and finally lost to the French—went their best station for this purpose.

Thus, when the seventeenth century was three-quarters past, the Dutch were overmastered in both North and South Atlantic waters. What they retained—Guiana and Curaçao—in actual possession did not make up for these very heavy losses.

Had the Dutch not reduced into possession the whole of the Portuguese Empire in the East and Far East, their position would now have been a very insignificant one, for their settlement at the Cape represented very much what St. Helena and Ascension now do for British shipping.

For a century and a quarter after the fall of New Amsterdam the old order of things continued, and then the French Revolution broke out, bringing with it the most astounding changes of fortune for Holland and her Colonial Empire.

During all this time the Dutch were undisturbed in their distant possessions in the Pacific. Spain and Portugal had dropped out of the running; France and England were fiercely stabbing each other wherever they could—chiefly in Canada and India— and left the Dutch alone.

As the time of the Revolution drew near, however, it began to be seen that France had had the worst of the long struggle. In North America, indeed, she was a little more than quits; if she had been expelled from Canada, she was chiefly instrumental in expelling England from the rest of the Continent. But her losses in India remained unavenged; there was nothing to set off against the ruin of all her gorgeous schemes of Eastern Empire.

Moreover, it was plain that even in the West Indies her position was most insecure.

Such was the situation of France; she was still eager, still ambitious, although constantly baffled. We shall see how she made two tremendous bids for a world empire before the Great Peace. In the meantime, we may profitably consider the use that Holland made of this long period of untroubled Eastern rule. I have ventured the position that the Empire of Holland was a miracle of shopkeeping. It is not intended to imply that there is anything to be deplored in an empire being conducted on sound business principles. On the contrary, it is better that it should be so: certainly far better for the happiness of its subjects that the dominant idea of empire should be that of peaceful development rather than of rapacious warfare.

Nevertheless, there are degrees of devotion to gain. The English, who are continually denounced as shopkeepers — men, that is, who have no sense of responsibility towards their Eastern fellow-subjects, and look on their vast dominions as so many estates to be exploited for the greatest possible advantage of England, and of England alone — may profitably study the records of the largest shop ever kept—the Dutch Empire. It was an extensive and complicated business. It will be impossible to do more here than to glance at a single incident which is typical.

The Dutch owned, as we have seen, the two islands of Ceylon and Java. These islands have no imaginable connection, racial or geographical, and they are separated by about 1,500 miles of sea. Their material interests must necessarily be entirely unconnected. Fate brought them both under the yoke of Holland. Their new masters did indeed study local conditions with some attention, but it was in order that they might make the greatest possible profit for themselves, not in order that they might administer each island to the greatest advantage of its inhabitants.

The great difficulty in Ceylon was the rice supply, which was always short, and sometimes brought the Cingalese perilously near to a famine. Rice is a wet crop, and often requires for its cultivation irrigation works that are much beyond the power of the ordinary farmer to carry out. Building tanks, for instance, cutting canals and damming streams. These works are throughout the East regarded as proper objects for Government care. The native rulers of Ceylon had done, if not their duty, at any rate something towards this work. We should expect to find the Dutch energetically taking up the work, and making up for lost time as quickly as possible.

The Dutch, however, did nothing of the kind. They did not construct new tanks, nor repair those that the ravages of war had damaged; they allowed tanks to fall into disuse wherever possible. We wonder at so cruel a line of policy until we realize that it is all simply a matter of business. The sufferings of the Cingalese were nothing to the Dutch; they were not there to please the Cingalese. As for rice, that was a Java crop; and an immense population of half-starving Cingalese was the best possible market for the Java houses; they made vast fortunes out of every scarcity.

It would certainly have served no useful purpose to waste large sums of money in constructive works in Ceylon, the only effect of which would have been to lower the profits of the Java houses; that would not have been at all good business. In Ceylon itself the Dutch made money out of cinnamon; so it was clearly understood that Java was to serve the rice ring, and Ceylon the cinnamon ring.

It would hardly be precise to describe this course of action as cynical; for the Dutch, with all their virtues, do not appear to have had a glimmer of an idea that there could be any higher duties connected with their position than to make as much money as possible out of it.

But it is, nevertheless, a most extraordinary example of heartless manipulation of the interests of great populations to the advantage of a few capitalists. When England grows conscience-stricken as to whether she is really doing her duty by India, it might be comforting to read for a while the records of Holland's work. It is not savage cruelty of the Spanish type that we encounter in Dutch administration, it is only a dull and sordid tyranny. Of course, every great empire has its characteristic vices as well as virtues. The Dutch were pacific, but in revenge they were relentlessly greedy of money. The time was coming when this immense fabric was to be broken up from its foundations.

On January 27, 1795, the Stadtholderate was declared to be abolished, and the Batavian Republic established. The Prince of Orange fled from Holland, and was accommodated with apartments in Hampton Court Palace. By the middle of April the English withdrew the forces that they opposed in Holland to the advance of the Revolutionary forces.

Holland was virtually absorbed into the French Republic, just as one hundred and fifteen years earlier Portugal had been absorbed into Spain. The immense territory over-seas that was known as the Dutch East Indies, together with the Cape of Good Hope and Ceylon, fell into French hands, and became the natural prey of those with whom France was at war.

Such measure as Holland had meted out to Portugal might now be expected to be measured to her again by England. Ruthlessly and relentlessly had Holland despoiled Portugal, and she now herself fell into the clutches of a Power that is incessantly denounced as greedy and grasping.

On September 23 the Cape fell. The commander-in-chief of the expedition bore a letter of recommendation from the Prince of Orange desiring that there might be no resistance, but it was disregarded.

Already in August the English had conquered Malacca. On February 15, 1796,

Ceylon was captured. In the next year the wealthy prize of the Moluccas fell into our hands; three years later we reduced Dutch Guiana, and in the following year Curaçao. There remained to Holland nothing but Java, and even Java was isolated and cut off from communication with Europe.

The empire of Holland was now indeed in a parlous state. The mother-country, as the Batavian Republic, was in dependence (thinly disguised as alliance) on her powerful neighbour, France. Abroad all was lost, East and West, the route to the East gone, and Java only remaining Dutch. Even Java must soon fall in the natural course of events.

At the beginning of the nineteenth century an observant Dutchman must have felt that there was little hope of a revival of his country's greatness. There could be no more rings in cinnamon, rice or coffee—at any rate, for Dutchmen. The days were gone for ever when fat fortunes could be laid up by the sweating of Javanese or Cingalese. The outlook was hopeless; for into whose hands had the Dutch Empire fallen? Into the hands of England.

Nevertheless, at the Peace of Amiens, concluded in the year 1802, the entire area of the conquered Dutch Empire was restored to Holland with the one exception of Ceylon; no doubt there are many who think that we ought to have restored Ceylon also.

To appreciate the true bearing of this course of action we must endeavour to realize what was the situation of England at this time. The war that closed at the Peace of Amiens had been from the outset directed, on the part of France, to securing the route to the East. This was doubly secured by France; she held the Cape route by virtue of the Dutch 'alliance,' and the Egyptian expedition of Napoleon was to secure the Mediterranean route. There is no doubt whatever of her objective; although in our fathers' days there were many who held that there was no proof of the Emperor's animosity to England. Dazzled perhaps by the second empire, they maintained that our grandfathers' view of Napoleon was a mere craze, and that we should have done better to ally ourselves with him.

What chance there would have been of our alliance being accepted we can see from the correspondence of the time. 'As for Egypt,' the Minister for Foreign Affairs wrote to Buonaparte on September 23, 1797, 'as a colony it would supplement the products of the West Indies, and as a route it would give us the commerce of India; in business, time is everything, and the time saved would give us five voyages instead of three only by the ordinary route.' The ordinary route was the route round the Cape of Good Hope.

At that time, of course, the Cape had already passed away from French control; but the way in which they regarded the Dutch possessions is well illustrated by these lines from Buonaparte to the Minister of Foreign Affairs, September 13, 1797: 'Supposing that at the general peace we were obliged to restore the Cape of Good Hope to England, we should then have to seize Egypt.' Neither the Minister nor the

General makes a pretence that the Cape of Good Hope is to be regarded as anything but French ground. This, then, was the situation : France was making two determined attempts to get at India, stretching one long arm round the south of Africa, and thrusting another along the Mediterranean to seize Egypt and the Red Sea. Both attempts were defeated ; the first by the simple capture of the Cape of Good Hope ; the second in a more complicated manner. The battle of the Nile shut up the French in Egypt, and cut them off from France ; the capture of Malta and Minorca confirmed our grip on the route eastwards, and the march of Baird through the desert with his Indian army completed the disaster.

When the time came for making peace, both routes to the East had fallen into our hands, and both were surrendered. This may be called ignorant, or short-sighted, or cowardly, but it cannot with any show of reason be called greedy. The menace to India was as plainly demonstrated as any policy can be ; and yet we were contented to run that terrible risk a second time. We made only two reservations. The first was Ceylon. The campaign of Suffren had proved what havoc might be wrought to India by a hostile fleet possessing a base in that island. As the Dutch were plainly unable to defend themselves against the French, to retain Ceylon was the smallest measure of self-defence that we could take. Accordingly we retained Ceylon; we simply did not dare to leave so strong an outpost to India in such feeble hands. All the rest of the conquered Dutch Empire was restored to Holland; as to which all that can be said is that it was a piece of extravagant generosity.

The only reservation that we made in Europe was as regards Malta. Egypt we evacuated; Minorca we evacuated. As to Malta, all that we asked was a material guarantee that it would not be occupied by the French as soon as our backs were turned. The guarantee was not given, and war broke out again. There are Englishmen who hold that the guarantee never ought to have been demanded; and that throughout the negotiations England behaved very badly to Napoleon, who meekly endured our exactions until he was pushed beyond endurance.

This point is a little beside our subject; but the fact remains that when the last stage of the great struggle commenced, it found Holland once more a world-power. Unless we start with the assumption that England cannot under any circumstances do a good deed, and that what would be generous in another power is merely selfish or crafty in England, we shall have to conclude that the revived Empire of Holland was a free gift from England. The war broke out again then, and the processes of the earlier war were repeated. Surinam was captured in 1804, the Cape of Good Hope in 1806, Curaçao in 1807, the Moluccas in 1810, Java in 1811. This time the conquest was complete; not an acre remained to Holland outside Europe. We are to observe, further, that these conquests, with the exception of Surinam, were made from France direct, and not from Holland. Early in the year 1806 Louis Buonaparte was formally proclaimed

King of Holland. The entire extent of the Dutch Empire became French soil, and as legitimately open to English attack as the Portuguese Empire had been to the attack of Holland when Portugal was conquered by Spain.

In the earlier war there had been at first some hesitation on the part of England. The situation was equivocal; for we were not at war with Holland. The Stadtholder was the guest of George III., and recommended his officers to hand over their provinces to England. Later on, the situation cleared up, as the Dutch refused to follow their Stadtholder's advice. In the second war the situation was, almost from the outset, clearly defined. For the second time in the course of ten years, Holland suffered the fate of Portugal; her Empire was engulfed in that of a powerful neighbour.

On this occasion not even Java held out; and for the second time the Dutch Empire was in the grasp of England, who restored the entire area to Holland with the exception of the Cape of Good Hope. No doubt there are many who will hold that we ought to have restored the Cape of Good Hope also.*

We did not, however, do so; but kept in our own hands the control of the route to the East round the South of Africa. This was the only loss suffered by Holland at the Great Peace. To-day finds us also in Egypt, having taken close upon a hundred years to master our lesson.

We have now arrived at the last stage in the history of the Dutch Empire. If its rise and development were surprising, not less so were the closing episodes, which left it, as regards the Far East, intact after all its vicissitudes.

The Colonial Empire of Holland is the sole considerable Empire of the modern world that has a continuous history since its foundation. Batavia, founded in the year 1619 as the capital of the East Indies, is the capital of the Dutch East Indies to-day, and the area of the Dutch Empire

* England, having conquered the Cape of Good Hope from Louis Buonaparte, paid Holland six millions sterling for the privilege of retaining that conquest and Guiana.

there has not shrunk in the course of three centuries.

The present Colonial Empire of France, vast in extent though it is, is a creation of this century only—even of the last half century. With the exception of the French West Indies, it has but a very short history. The Empires of Spain and Portugal are so sadly shrunken—the one in consequence of extravagant misgovernment, the other in consequence of dreadful disasters—that it is hardly fair to compare them with the great and wealthy possessions of Holland, although the Portuguese possess in Goa, and the Spaniards in Santiago de Cuba, a link with a more distant past even than the foundation of Batavia.

That Holland should occupy to-day the unique and very favourable position of a small nation ruling a considerable empire, is owing to the fact that she had the good luck to fall into the hands of England. It was not that she had an overflowing population, for she remained to the end a little people. It was not that her stock was more martial than that of her rivals, for her colonies fell at once and almost without a struggle over and over again.

The Dutch Empire had very little resisting power; it was swallowed up by France as easily as Portugal was swallowed up by Spain. But the Portuguese Empire was exposed by its misfortunes to the assault of a Power flushed with successful rebellion, and just entering on its course of expansion, whereas when the turn of Holland came, she fell into the hands of a Power that was too grand and mighty to care about unsought additions to her possessions. We have also to note the long period of peaceful development enjoyed by Holland; this was not enjoyed by her because she was stronger than her foes, but because France and England were perpetually at war, and unable to make any great efforts outside the two classic arenas of their conflict—Canada and India.

In the dealings of England with the Dutch Empire we no doubt come across a great deal of blameworthy ignorance as to its value.

But even in that ignorance there is a certain nobility. Besides, when we say that England was ignorant of what she was restoring, that is only one part of the story. Our ministers may have been unaware of the value of the colonies that they were handing back to Holland, but they were quite aware that they were being asked, and pressingly asked, to hand back something. They failed in their duty departmentally, by not making more sure of what they were doing.

But, however we may distribute personal blame, there still remains the extraordinary fact (the fact so important to Holland) that her empire was twice handed back to her when (especially the second time) she could hardly have expected to regain any portion of it.

What led England into a course without example in history will always be a matter of dispute. Some there will be who will affirm that England deserves no credit for declining to despoil a defenceless neighbour, her action being simply the outcome of departmental inadvertence. Others will maintain that it was from a genuine desire not to impoverish an old friend that we relinquished the Dutch Indies, East and West, and that our action was a very generous one.

But whether the mainspring of our action towards Holland was indifference or generosity, it is submitted that it certainly was not greed.

VI.
CONCLUSIONS.

VI.

CONCLUSIONS.

THE British Empire is not lost yet. But there is no reason why it should not be if it is sufficiently mismanaged. It was not founded by a miracle; and we must not expect that a miracle will ever be wrought to conserve it. Hence the value to Englishmen of the study of empires that have in the past been won and lost.

The situation of England at the present moment is exactly analogous to that of Portugal immediately before her collapse. Portugal had no men; England has no food. For a whole generation before the disaster of 1580 it was becoming increasingly plain, year by year, that unless some governmental measure were adopted to keep men in Portugal, the steady drain of men to the East would at last bring about a crisis. That crisis would be nothing more nor less than this: that Portugal might be overflowingly rich, and yet completely defenceless. The necessary measures were not taken, and Portugal fell in a fortnight. Had time been granted her she could have made a respectable defence, but Spain had no intention of throwing away so valuable an opportunity, and time was not granted to Portugal.

In England it has been growing increasingly plain, for the last twenty years at least, that unless some governmental measure were adopted to get grain into the country and keep it there, the time would come when the country would be within measurable distance of starvation. The time has come. It is not a question of whether this or that Power or combination of Powers would be malicious enough to cut off our supplies. We need not discuss the question as one of hostile import if we do not wish to do so; for the situation would be almost the same if a universal treaty of arbitration were in full operation. The point is, that by the failure of two harvests there would not be food enough on the planet. It would not be a question of England being able to get at it or not; the food would not be there.

The obvious remedy is, since we have so much good wheat country, to grow the food ourselves. But for some reason England is doggedly opposed to doing anything of the kind. It is one of the most singular crazes known to history. Future historians will make infinite merriment over a nation that called itself practical, and yet pursued a policy that at one and the same time made it the most envied nation in the world, and cut off all its sources of the first indispensable material of war.

For it is not that food is among the necessary munitions of war: it is the first and indispensable munition of war. Having got our men, we must feed them before they can fight; surely that is the A B C of warfare.

The cheap and easy task of describing what would happen if some unfriendly Power chose a time of scarcity to declare war has been so often performed that it is unnecessary to perform it again here. But surely writers on that subject take too roseate a view of what would happen to England under those circumstances. It is generally assumed that by paying a sum of money—one thousand millions, two thousand millions, or some colossal sum—we could put an end to our miseries.

Such a stipulation would be a waste of paper and ink; for one thousand millions could as easily be extracted from Iceland as from England with her empire gone. Any power that had the good luck to get her fingers round England's throat in this way would not be so foolish as to let the opportunity slip of throttling her once and for ever. We saw what Philip did to Portugal when the opportunity came for which he had so long waited. Supposing the worst possible to have happened, and England, with her forty millions of starving folk, to be ringed round with hostile cruisers.

The enemy would be lacking in common

sense if he helped us out of our difficulties, for he would not get such an opportunity again. That such a course would be 'inhumane' is saying very little to the purpose. 'When I go to war,' said the grim old Marshal, 'I pack up my humanity, and leave it behind with my wife's kit.' Perhaps the enemy might go so far as to relieve our distress to the extent of 'assisting emigration' to what would then have become her colonies.

These are gloomy reflections. But they were stern realities (substituting 'men' for 'food') to Portugal three hundred years ago, and there is, in the nature of things, no reason why they should not become realities for England. Our case is exactly analogous. With time we could, of course, get out of our difficulties; but time is precisely that which will not be allowed to us, any more than it was to Portugal.

The usual reply (when these considerations are urged) is that this Power or the other 'would never' take a course of action that would entail a disagreeable consequence to herself—temporary loss of trade for example. Considering the immense value of the British Empire there are surely several nations who would gladly suffer not only a slight and temporary, but a very substantial loss for the purpose of helping to loot us, and would be amply repaid if they succeeded.

No doubt the same things were said in Portugal when any 'alarmist' pointed out the Spanish danger. Two such faithful sons of the Church 'would never' fall out; neighbours who had learnt for many centuries to know and respect each other 'would never' have a difference that could not be amicably adjusted; their external interests were perfectly distinct, one to the East, the other to the West, under the award of the Holy Father.

Latterly, especially, since Portugal had shown herself so militantly orthodox, the countries had drawn much closer; orthodox Philip could not but respect and admire a country that showed such praiseworthy zeal for the good cause. Finally, the material interest of Spain, plainly, was to keep

Portugal intact. Quite apart from spiritual or racial affinities, the mere promptings of self-interest would deter Spain from breaking up the whole fabric of the Eastern trade. She 'would never' dislocate an entire system of commercial connection from which she herself derived so much benefit with no greater advantage in view than the acquisition of more territory, when she had too much already.

'Was für Plunder!' sighed old Blucher with tears of regret in his eyes as from the peaceful vantage ground of S. Paul's Cathedral he surveyed the City of London. 'Was für Plunder!' says the world of to-day, but with more of anticipation than regret in her voice, as she surveys the vast and wealthy extent of the British Empire.

But we lose sight of things as they are when we assume that nations only go to war from nicely-balanced reasonings of self-interest. It is mostly from outbreaks of popular passion, unreasoned anger unreasonably insisted in, that modern nations go to war. Cabinets are, in fact, a good deal hampered in resisting impulses of this kind on the ground that the war is not to the nation's interest; for in declaring war they always have to make out that it is with the utmost reluctance that they find themselves driven to advise their master to take such an awful measure. The catchword varies in every case—the honour of the flag, the fatherland, the cause of orthodoxy—these are some; but never self-interest. In being told that our friends 'would never' do anything so contrary to their own interest as to declare war against England we are being told that they 'would never' do that which, as a matter of fact, every nation professes to be doing when she goes to war.

Portugal fell by reason of ignoring facts that were glaringly obvious. The food supply is one such in the case of England. Another is, that there are too many people in England and too few in the Colonies. England could easily spare a few millions; the Colonies could as easily swallow them up—even more easily if they rightly understood their interests. The statesman who should set a current of immigration flowing into the vast waste-lands of the South would do more to strengthen and enrich the Colonies than the discovery of a gold-mine could effect.

There is one other source of strength that Englishmen possess, of which, so natural does it seem to her, she would never be conscious unless by studying the lost empire of Portugal: it is that they do not mix freely with their Eastern fellow-subjects. This is often made a reproach to them, with the usual adjectives, haughty, unsympathetic, and others more severe still.

But we have but to see how grave was the diminution of force that the abounding sympathy of Portugal brought to her, to recognize at once what a source of strength to us is our so-called haughtiness, which is really nothing more than instinctive common-sense.

The contemplation of the lost empire of Spain ought to be one of unmixed consolation to England; for we have avoided all the mistakes that Spain made. We are so accustomed to our own attitude of complete toleration of all the creeds (some so strange to us) of our empire, that we have come to look on toleration as the rule, and intolerant action as the exception. That is an entire mistake. Spain was grossly intolerant; so, in her decadence, was Portugal; France half strangled her own promising colony of Canada by shutting out all immigrants except those of one faith. We should do well to remember, now and then, how inexhaustible is the source of strength to the empire implied in the word toleration.

It is quite a delusion to suppose that persecution always fails. If applied with sufficient vigour and relentlessness, it is often completely successful. The crushed worm does not turn if you tread hard enough. But it is, after all, only a very narrow kind of success — from the point of view of this world—that can be attained by persecution. If 'success' is held to imply the stamping of one form of religious belief on the minds of the people, that measure of success can be attained. In this sense Spain was completely successful. But if we inquire the price of her success, we shall find that it was a price that England will never be persuaded to pay; for it is the moral and intellectual ruin of the people. Besides these considerations, the material ruin of the people is an inconsiderable incident; but that, too, follows in most cases.

With our awakened sense of the illuminating value of history, and the great importance of a knowledge of the past as a guide to the present and the future, we cannot help feeling that the scrupulously careful conduct of England in the East is a legitimate source of pride. Let us consider what the Spaniard destroyed, and what the Englishman has preserved. Temples, legends, faiths, languages almost, customs, creeds, all the varied and intensely picturesque and instructive incidents of an old civilization—all were shrivelled up in the devastating breath of the Spanish fury. All have been religiously preserved and protected by England to the utmost of her power. Cavillers will say that this is no more than our duty. Granted—fully granted:

but the Spaniard thought that he was doing his duty also. The question is, Whose sense of duty is the higher?

There is nothing that is French that may not be studied with profit; not even the French Colonial Empire. We are accustomed to remember with complacency that we owe nothing, or next to nothing, to our ministers, and that our own empire contrasts favourably with others like it, chiefly because it is almost entirely the work of the people. No doubt: but we may profitably consider how much the French achieved, in spite of the difficulties caused by an almost complete lack of popular support. For England it would appear that, just at present, and in several directions, the questions awaiting decision are precisely those that can be solved by the patient consideration of experts rather than by popular impulses. Let us remember, then, how nearly French intelligence beat us out of Canada, with all our numbers in our favour. There are several most important policies awaiting settlement that are absolutely incapable of solution except by conferences of experts, who will bring trained intelligence to bear on the tangled web of conflicting interests.

Impulse is invaluable while empires are being made; but in later stages intelligence is indispensable. Intelligence will but rarely make a country expand into an empire; but no work of consolidation can be achieved without a very liberal measure of intelligent and concerted effort.

The most difficult task for the conscientious hesitator—one sometimes fears that it is an impossible task—is to bring himself into that state of mind in which the Commons of England resolved that 'Robert, Lord Clive, hath at the same time rendered great and meritorious services to his country.' If he really merit the name of 'conscientious,' let him in conscience' name study the Lost Empire of France. Let him remember Champlain perpetually kept in the background, De la Salle unsupported, Bussy thwarted, Labourdonnais dying of a broken heart, Dupleix neglected and ruined, Lally dragged through the streets of Paris on a hurdle; and let him remember that Canada and India were lost to France because of these misdeeds, wrought, for the most part, in the solemn name of justice.

When we have the good fortune to have a great man among us, let us at least be great enough ourselves to know him for what he is. If we are looking for a great man who is blameless, we are looking for the Messiah. But we can find plenty of men among us who are neither great nor blameless: they are the common stuff of humanity. Although there is something intensely gratifying to ordinary mankind in catching a great man tripping, it is not really a grand discovery that we have made. All men make slips, but most men are small enough to conceal them. The truly grand attitude of mind is reached when, having judged, men can bring themselves to say that 'Robert, Lord Clive, hath at the same time rendered great and meritorious services to his country.'

It has not been possible, within the limits of this volume, to give more than a hint of the way in which Holland regarded her

Colonial Empire; the entire volume would be too scanty a space to devote to that most instructive study. It would show Englishmen how far a great people—a really great people—can misapprehend the nature of an empire. As in every other way, we are continually being reminded how far short we fall in the task of 'doing our duty' to our fellow subjects. No doubt we do fall short: but, at any rate, we acknowledge that we have a duty; and that is more than Holland ever recognized. If we do not do so much as we might do towards increasing their happiness and prosperity, we do, at any rate, admit that their happiness and prosperity is our goal; and not the enrichment of Englishmen by every possible means, and at any cost of suffering to those subjects of the Empress who are not Englishmen. Base though this aim may be that (as we justly pride ourselves) is not ours, it was nevertheless the aim of a nation that we are continually exhorted to admire and bow down to.

Those who think about the British Empire at all fall roughly into four classes:

1. The Jingoes.
2. The reasonable Imperialists.
3. The conscientious hesitator.
4. The Little Englanders.

In good times the second class outnumbers all the others put together, but not very largely, and in troubled times the Jingoes are a dead weight, and the Little Englanders a danger. The balance is decided by the attitude of the conscientious hesitators, who are drawn upwards or downwards by all sorts of considerations, but who are constitutionally open to the very able appeals that the Little Englanders make to their conscience.

These determined foes of our country, numerically insignificant, are powerful by reason of their pertinacity and recklessness, and by the influence that they exercise over the hesitators. Their appeals are most adroitly made, and are always covered by that most attractive mask, the mask of noble and unselfish aims. They are never abashed, never disconcerted, never discouraged, and it would not be accurate to say that they do not mind what damage they cause, for their object is to cause damage. Their grand source of strength is the ignorance of their dupes, an ignorance which is not to be wondered at, nor easily overcome, for no questions are so complicated as those of Imperial policy, and some are only fit to be debated by experts. Nevertheless, they are all thrown into the arena of party strife: that is one of the drawbacks to our otherwise successful method of government.

With this exception, and also with the exception of the dangers noted earlier in this chapter, the story of the lost empires is of rather favourable omen than otherwise to the British Empire of to-day. As a rule, the first sign of an empire's decline is the failing vitality of the parent stock. Never before in our history have we been so variously and so healthily active as at the present moment. The vitality of England appears to be not only sustained at a high level, but to be exuberant, inexhaustible. The nation has even undergone unscathed the severe test of twenty-five years' education. There are weak points, no doubt, here and there, but none—beyond those already indicated—that seem likely to become malignant dangers—none, at any rate, at home.

Abroad there are some that may be very dangerous indeed. In India there are two, one affecting the Civil Service, the other the Army. The army has been treated with particular cruelty, but it is one of the most re-assuring features of our political system that abuses are not permanently overlooked. It may take a long time to fix upon them the requisite amount of attention to secure their remedy; but the remedy is in the end secured, although, perhaps, more slowly than under a more vigorous administration.

The position of the Civil Service is peculiar. Next to the Army it is the chief pillar of Anglo-Indian rule. Forty years ago it was not supposed to be overpaid, and yet in the last forty years pay has fallen sixty per cent., owing to the fall in silver; prices have risen perhaps forty per cent., and the work has trebled. There is no fear that Englishmen will not always get through as much work as they possibly can, whether their pay be magnificent or barely sufficient. But every man has his tether, and if he has to spend his time in mountains of correspondence his time is gone, and it may be open to question whether it has been spent to the best advantage. That was a fine phrase, that every Englishman should bear himself in the East like an Ambassador of the Empress— a perfect definition indeed; but who ever heard of an Ambassador in a hurry? and when was a modern civilian in anything but a hurry?

The drift of this observation, of course, is that so much of our authority in the East depends on the personal contact of English and Asiatic. It was this that inspired Sir John Malcolm's instruction to the service that they should live, in the Eastern phrase, 'with four doors open': be of perfectly easy access to every native; for to listen to a man is sometimes as good as granting him what he prays for. All this invaluable personal intercourse must of necessity be restricted or, which is as bad, hurried over, if a man is nervously anxious to finish his last report on a scheme that need never have been promulgated. That invaluable basis of our influence, perfect mastery of the native tongues, must needs be weakened if office work is so heavy. These are not fatal weaknesses, but they are weaknesses. They tend to enfeeble the grip of the district officer over his district. The East is the same as it always was, and the Oriental does not understand the man in authority being hurried like an overworked telegraph clerk. He likes to see his great man take his ease affably, and will not approach him at all unless he can get a few minutes' easy chat.

If the work has increased the pay has diminished. There are only two ways of paying men—in money or in honour. The money pay is less than half what it was, and for honour, by which is here meant decorations, and all the little points of precedence and formality that are as the breath of their nostrils to some men, Englishmen as a rule care nothing at all. It would perhaps be more accurate to say that they profess to care nothing at all, whereas in reality they care a great deal. This insincere attitude of mind is due partly to the grapes having so long been sour—English decorations until quite recently having been very scarce and reserved for grandees. It is partly due also to the misunderstood teachings of some social prophets. There remains the Englishman's preference for substantial reward, which forms the residuum of a feeling that is probably on the decrease on the whole. It still persists, however, and makes one more difficulty when we come to consider how to get the superlatively good work of the civil service for about one-half of the proper pay. That illustrious service, once standing so high in honour and emolument, is now greatly shrunken in both. Yet it is to a great extent on the efficiency of that service that the British Empire in India rests.

As to foreign attacks, there is scarcely a doubt that, sooner or later, it will come. Into the struggle for empires all nations have now entered, some of whom are quite unfitted for empire even if they achieved it, and some are of already demonstrated incapacity.

Nevertheless, they will not be left behind in the race if they can help it. The greater reason for England to be, more than ever, the strong man armed. The greater reason for her to be of one mind, so far as possible, so that when the hour of conflict strikes, the trumpet shall give out no uncertain sound. Then there will be, at least in our days, no lost empire of England. But there might have been had our foes struck twelve years ago. Twelve years ago there is hardly a doubt that we might have been 'rushed' successfully. It was not that the army was weak, for it is always weak; it was not that the navy was lamentably below strength: it was that the very soul of the nation seemed sick. We seemed to have neither heart nor head left to us. Every form of sentimentalism raged abroad unchecked; the voice of common-sense was drowned; the people seemed bewitched. We lived in an inverted world; duty was derided, loyalty was a superstition, war a wickedness, the law of the land an intolerable burden.

Then came the crash in Egypt; the

campaign of 'almost mythic grandeur' in the Soudan, and the tragedy of Khartoum; and still the people babbled on.

At the height of the brabble the voice of a Cambridge professor made itself slowly heard. In language of frozen impartiality he bade us remember what were the issues of which we talked so lightly; what were the tremendous interests that we were preparing, as the phrase went, to 'throw into the cauldron.' Under this exhortation men looked eastward to the Soudan, where the rule of the Khalifa reminded them of the consequences of duty forgotten and responsibility shirked. Perhaps, after all, there might be something to be said for the old teaching of home and school that for Englishmen duty comes first.

Men looked at home; and some phrases that once sounded so alluring sounded hollow to their ears. Some reputations, once so high, seemed overrated; some figures that once loomed so large to their eyes flickered and grew dim and unsteady, as if seen through a bloody mist.

As the sense of individual duty towards the millions who dwell under the sceptre of the Empress grew stronger, the nation grew less flighty. Times mended; and, from the year of Jubilee onwards, the chances of the foes of the empire have grown yearly slighter and more uncertain. But let us not, in our revived sense of security, forget where honour is due. Let us not fail to remember that thousands who now give a loyal and sometimes clamorous applause to the Imperial ideal, owe their inspiration (although perhaps unconsciously) to the genius of Sir John Seeley.

INDEX.

ABERCROMBIE, GENERAL, 226
Abraham, Heights of, battle, 216
Abyssinian Expedition, 56
Abyssinia, Prime Minister of, 60
Aden, held by Portuguese, 67
Affonso, King, 43
Africa, Portuguese in, 9
Africa, West Coast of, 298, 305
Agincourt, Henry of, 47
Aix-la-Chapelle, Treaty of, 216
Akbar, 98, 238
Albuquerque, 80
Alexander the Great, 236
Algarves, 45, 49
Almagro, 141, 159
Alva, 294
Amherst, 227
Amiens, Peace of, 319
Anahuac, 120
Arcot, Defence of, 251
Aryan races, 36
Ascension Isle, 311
Asia, Central, 16, 42
Atahuallpa, Emperor, 153, 161
Auchmuty, Sir Samuel, 281
Aurangabad, 258, 265
Aviz, John of, 45
Aztecs, The, 111

Baird, Sir David, 281

Baird's march through the desert, 321
Bajazet, 166
Barillon, 206
Bastile, Labourdonnais in, 248
Batavia, 325
Batavian Republic, 316
Bengal, English expelled from, 260
Bijapur, 74, 81, 238
Blucher, 339
Bojador, Cape, 51
Bonrepaux, 206
Borneo, 289
Braddock, General, 221
Bradstreet, 227
Brazil, Discovery of, 73
Brazil, Empire of, 32, 71, 305
Brazil, Republic of, 8, 71
Brazilians, Loyalty of, 83
Brazils, The, 310
Breton, Cape, 216, 222
Breton, Cape, Capture of, 226
Brissac, Marshal de, 177
British Empire, 2, 6, 7, 17, 26, 33, 70, 76, 236, 333, 339, 347, 353
Briton, Early, 35
Brooke, Rajah, 69
Burgundy, Henry of, 43

INDEX

Bussy, Marquis de, 240, 250, 257, 277, 345
Byng, Admiral, 269

Cabral, Pedro Alvares, 72
Cadamosto, 60
Cairo, 58
Calicut, Rajah of, 71
Caliphate, 39
Callao, 139
Camoens, 37
Canada, 19, 196, 202, 283, 311
Canada, First English expedition against, 194
Cananore, 58
Canary Islands, 52
Cape Bojador, 51
Cape of Good Hope, 64, 290, 302, 311, 317, 320, 323
Cape of Good Hope, Capture of, by England, 281
Cape of St. Vincent, 48
Cape Verde, Discovery of, 54
Carlos, King, 46
Carolina, South, 209
Cartier, Jacques, 188
Cataraqui Fort, Capture of, by England, 227
Caxamalca, 154
Celebes, The, 290, 302
Central America, 297
Central Asia, 16, 42
Ceuta, 47
Ceylon, 290, 313, 317, 322
Chamfort, M. de, 29
Champlain, Lake, 216
Champlain, marriage of, 189
Champlain, Samuel, 177, 203, 345
Chandanagar, 241
Charles I. of England, 196
Charles V., 148, 156
Chateauneuf, M. de, 195
Chesterfield, Lord, 255
China, 165, 188, 203
Choiseul, 270, 272
Cholula, 123
Cintra, Gonsalo de, 53

Clinton, Governor of New York, 219
Clive, Robert, 90, 242, 251, 345, 346
Cochrane, 245
Colbert, 200
Colonial Empire of France, 18
Colonial Empire of Portugal, 8
Columbus, Christopher, 62
Condé, Prince de, 180, 191
Constantinople, 42
Coote, Eyre, 263, 267, 277, 281
Coromandel Coast, 245, 277
Cortez, Hernando, 74, 104, 149
Covilham, 57
Cromwell's Navigation Laws, 309
Crown Point, 227
Cuba, 12, 107, 126, 234
Curaçao, 235, 290, 310, 318, 323

D'Aché, 240, 257, 266
D'Aumont, Marshal, 177
Deccan, The, 250, 258
De Mont, 188
Diaz, Diniz, 53, 63
D'Iberville, 205
Drake, 85
Dupleix, 240, 241, 345
Duquesne, Fort, 219, 228
Dutch East Indies, 8
Dutch settlements in America, 202

Early Britons, 35
Ecuador, 142
Edward III. of England, 47
Egypt, 22, 321, 322, 354
Emirs of Portugal, 40
Empire of Brazil, 32, 71
Empire, British, 2, 6, 7, 17, 26, 33, 70, 76, 236, 333, 339, 347, 353
Empire, First modern European, 8
Empire of France, 6, 17, 21, 25, 93, 173, 236, 240, 281, 282

INDEX 359

Empire, French Indian, 22
Empire of Holland, 6, 22, 26, 93, 289, 329
Empire of Portugal, 6, 8, 9, 25, 33, 34, 44, 54, 66, 70, 75, 77, 89, 99, 174, 295, 311, 324, 326
Empire of Spain, 6, 13, 15, 25, 97-169, 174, 295, 326, 341
England, Queen of, 46
Etruria, Kingdom of, 230
Europe, Turkey in, 41

Ferdinand, Prince, 53
Fernandes, Alvaro, 54
Fleece, Golden, 46
Florida, French in, 183
Fontenoy, Battle of, 261
France, Empire of, 6, 17, 21, 25, 93, 173, 285
Francis I., 188
French Revolution, 311
Frontenac, Fort, 216, 224

Galissonnière, Comte de la, 215, 217
Gallo, Island of, 146
Gama, Vasco da, 64, 71
Gambia, 298
Ganges, River, 266
Garter, Knight of, 45, 46, 49
Gaunt, John of, 45
George III., 324
George, Lake, 217
Georgia, Colony of, 210
Godolphin, Lord, 206
Good Hope, Cape of, 64
Goree, 298, 302, 309
Government, Representative, 10
Guadeloupe, 234
Guatamozin, Emperor, 132, 133
Guiana, 310
Guinea Coast, 63

Haidar, 239, 273, 277, 281
Halifax, Foundation of, by England, 217

Hampton Court Palace, 316
Hastings, Warren, 242
Hebert, 180
Henry of Agincourt, 47
Henry of Burgundy, 43
Henry IV. of England, 45
Henry IV. of France, 177
Henry the Navigator, 32, 47, 69, 77, 175
Hispaniola, 106, 177
Holland, Empire of, 6, 22, 26, 93, 289, 329
Holmes, Robert, 207
Home Rule, 76
Howe, Viscount, 226
Hudson, Henry, 203
Hudson's Bay, English in, 202, 213
Hughes, Sir Edward, 276

Inca, Capture of the, 156
Inca, Death of the, 161
Inca, The, 13, 153
India, British, 235, 260, 262
India, Civil Service of, 350
India, Dutch in, 305
India, Foundation of French Empire, 243
India, French, 235, 240, 256, 259
India, Portuguese in, 9, 11
Indies, French, Dupleix, Governor of, 242
Inquisition, 86
Islam, 38, 41, 48, 97, 105, 167

James II., 39, 205
Jang, Sir Salar, 98, 239
Java, 289, 302, 313, 318, 323
Java, Capture of, by England, 281
Jesuits in Canada, 193
John III. of Portugal, 91
John of Aviz, 45
John of Gaunt, 45
John the Perfect, 32, 56, 60
Jonquière, De la, 218

Khartoum, 355
Kirk, David, 194, 204
Knight of the Garter, 45, 46, 49

Labourdonnais, 240, 245, 248, 345
Lally, 240, 250, 257, 260, 270, 345
La Salle, 197, 206, 211, 345
Lawrence, Major, 254
Law's scheme, 210
Leroy-Beaulieu, M., 173, 284
Lesseps, M. de, 178
Louis the Great, 20, 199
Louisburg, Fall of, 226
Louisburg, Fort, 217
Louisiana, State of, 200, 206, 228, 229

Macaulay, 237
Madagascar, 20, 58
Madeira, Discovery of, 51
Madras, Presidency of, 240, 263
Madras, Capitulation of, to France, 245
Magelhan, 161, 162
Mahdist revolt, 42
Mahomet, 42
Malacca, 302, 317
Malcolm, Sir John, 351
Malta, Capture of, by England, 321, 322
Manila, 163
Marlborough, Duke of, 255
Martinique, 234
Mauritius, 247
Mediterranean, 41, 321
Mexico, 103, 111
Mexico, Gulf of, 211, 228
Mexico, Lake of, 111
Middleton, Lord, 206
Minorca, 218, 321, 322
Mississippi, Discovery of, 163, 211
Mobile, Foundation of, 209
Moluccas, 290, 302, 318, 323
Montcalm, Marquis de, 223, 227
Montezuma, Emperor, 119

Montmorency, Duc de, 180, 192
Montreal, 216, 227
Moors, 45
Motley, 293
Murray, 228

Nadir, Shah, 99
Naples, Spanish influence in, 101
Napoleon, 20, 229, 281, 282, 323
Napoleon's attempt to secure the Mediterranean, 319
Narvaez, 128
Nasr-ad-Din Shah, 99
Navigator, Henry the, 32, 47, 69, 77, 175
Navigation Laws of Cromwell, 309
Nelson, Admiral, 274
New Amsterdam, 202, 207, 290, 307-309, 311
Newcastle, Duke of, 216
New Orleans, Foundation of, 210
New York, 207, 216, 309
Niagara Fort, 216, 224
Nile, Battle of the, 321
Normandy, William of, 43, 137
North America, 296, 305, 311
North America, Dutch Empire in, 309
North-West Passage, 203
Nova Scotia, 216, 221

Oglethorpe, Governor, 210
Ohio, 211, 218
Ontario, Lake, 207, 211, 224
Orange, Prince of, 316
Ormuz, 67
Oswego, 216, 223
Ovando, 105

Pacific, Dutch in the, 311
Panama, 139, 178
Panama, Vicar of, 140
Paraguay, 164
Paris, Treaty of, 271
Paton, 245
Payva, Affonso da, 57.

INDEX

Peninsular War, 13, 31, 93
Persia, 41
Peru, 103, 137, 151
Philip II., 120, 169
Philippines, 12
Phœnicia, 37
Pitt the Elder, 226, 229
Pittsburg, 227
Pizarro, Francis, 14, 74, 137, 149
Plassy, Battle of, 263
Pondicherry, 241, 262, 268
Porto Novo, Battle of, 278
Portugal, Emirs of, 40
Portugal, Empire of, 6, 8, 9, 25, 29-94, 99, 174, 295, 311, 324, 326
Portugal, Future of, 92
Prester John, Land of, 56
Provincial Assemblies, their attitude, 214, 228

Quebec, 177, 226
Quebec, capture by Kirk, 195
Quebec, Fall of, 216, 227

Rajah Brooke, 69
Rajah of Calicut, 71
Red Sea, The, 321
Representative Government, 10
Republic, Batavian, 316
Republic of Brazil, 8, 71
Revolt, Mahdist, 42
Revolution, French, 311
Richard III., 39
Richelieu, Duc de, 180, 194, 204
Rome, 36
Ryswick, Treaty of, 205

Sagres, 48
St. Germain-en-Laye, Treaty of, 196, 204
St. Helena, 311
St. Lawrence, 18, 188, 194, 206, 228
St. Vincent, Cape of, 48
St. Vincent, Lord, 275
Saracens, 38
Sati, Abolition of, 117
Sebastian, King of Portugal, 91

Seeley, Sir John, 356
Senegal, 298
Senegambia, 51
Seringapatam, Fall of, 241
Sicily, Spanish influence in, 101
Sluys, Battle of, 77
Sofala, 58
Soissons, Comte de, 180
Solyman, 98
Soto, De, 163, 209
Soudan, The, 355
Spain, Empire of, 6, 13, 15, 25, 97-169, 174, 295, 326, 341
Spanish South America, 14
Spice Islands, 298, 302
Straits of Magelhan, Discovery of, 162
Suffren, 240, 274, 322
Sumatra, 289
Sunderland, Earl of, 206
Surinam, Capture of, 323

Table Mountain, 64
Tadoussac, 185
Tangier, 47, 52
Tezcuco, King of, 120
Tezcuco, State of, 118
Thémines, Marquis de, 180, 191
Thinker, Henry the, 47
Ticonderoga, 227
Ticonderoga, Battle of, 226
Timúr, 166
Tippoo, Citoyen, 241
Tlascala, State of, 121, 123
Treaty of Paris, 271
Treaty of Ryswick, 205
Treaty of St. Germain-en-Laye, 196, 204
Treaty of Utrecht, 204
Treaty of Versailles, 273, 279, 284
Tristam, Nuño, 53
Tromp, Van, 301
Tunis, 51
Turkey in Europe, 41

United States of America, 165, 202

Utrecht, Treaty of, 204, 216, 221

Valverde, Father, 155
Vaudreuil, De, 220
Velasquez, Diego de, 107, 126
Ventadour, Duc de, 180, 192
Vera Cruz, 118
Verde, Cape, Discovery of, 54
Versailles, Treaty of, 273, 279, 284
Vignau, Nicholas, 189

Wandewash, Battle of, 268
War, Peninsular, 13, 31, 93
War, Seven Years', 259, 272
Wellington, Duke of, 31, 278
West Indian Islands, 305, 312
William Henry, Fort, 217
William of Normandy, 43, 137
Wolfe, General, 226, 227, 229

Zempoalla, 123
Zumarraga, Archbishop of Mexico, 117

THE END.

BILLING AND SONS, PRINTERS, GUILDFORD.
J. D. & Co.

www.ingramcontent.com/pod-product-compliance
Lightning Source LLC
Chambersburg PA
CBHW020225240426
43672CB00006B/421